To all the chefs, guests and wineries who have supported

Trattoria G

# TRATTORIA GRAPPOLO

## SIMPLE RECIPES FOR TRADITIONAL ITALIAN CUISINE

LEONARDO CURTI & JAMES O. FRAIOLI

Gibbs Smith, Publisher
TO ENRICH AND INSPIRE HUMANKIND
Salt Lake City | Charleston | Santa Fe | Santa Barbara

First Edition
11 10 09 08 07   5 4 3 2 1

Published by
Gibbs Smith, Publisher
P.O. Box 667
Layton, Utah 84041

Orders: 1.800.835.4993
www.gibbs-smith.com

Designed by Debra McQuiston
Printed and bound in Hong Kong

Library of Congress Cataloging-in-Publication Data
Curti, Leonardo.
  Trattoria grappolo : simple recipes for traditional italian cuisine /
Leonardo Curti and James O. Fraioli ; photographs by Luca Trovato
and Brian Hodges. — 1st ed.
      p. cm.
  Includes index.
  ISBN-13: 978-1-4236-0215-6
  ISBN-10: 1-4236-0215-3
  1. Cookery, Italian. 2. Trattoria Grappolo (Santa Ynez, Calif.) 3.
Wine and wine making. I. Fraioli, James O., 1968- II. Title.

TX723.C948 2007
641.5945—dc22
                          2007011261

Our high expectations for quality never exceed
the perfection of the ultimate purveyor, nature

# GRAPPOLO MAGIC

**WE ARE IN TRATTORIA GRAPPOLO** in downtown Santa Ynez, California, a scenic thirty-five minute drive north of Santa Barbara and two hours outside Los Angeles. The town is tranquil and dusty, signs of life reflect the days of the old west, where horses and carriages once pulled up to the hitching post for a hot meal and place to rest. But the spirited 90-seat bistro is also nestled amidst the richest wine-producing region of the state. It's no surprise Hollywood elected this bucolic town as the backdrop for the Academy Award nominated film *Sideways*.

For locals, Grappolo is *the* place to enjoy with friends and family. For visitors, particularly the throngs of wine tasters and Los Angeles mutineers who arrive to escape the city confines, Grappolo is the gateway to fun and excitement where a hive of activity abounds.

Surrounded by simple, rough-finish furnishings and mellow, persimmon-colored interior, Trattoria Grappolo flourishes with a wonderfully controlled chaos. Walk through the front door and a sumptuous aroma of freshly baked pizza and simmering tomato sauce teases the senses. The combination of the pastoral ambience of Italy with the lush vine fields and oak-studded hills of Santa Ynez helps create an ideal setting to serve up some of the most creative and authentic Italian dishes Central California has to offer.

"It's like a good party where everyone knows each other," says Leonardo Curti, his rolling accent revealing his Italian origin. "We want you to feel like you're at home." Meet Trattoria Grappolo's head chef and co-founder who, with younger brother Alfonso and business partner Daniele Serra, have taken the restaurant to new heights.

"People come here because they know what to expect," says Alfonso, a talented chef like his brother and whose specialties include Grappolo's rustic breads. The tall, debonair Italians attribute their culinary success to their mother, and their down-home dishes so popular with the diners prove

it. "There are no surprises—you get consistently great food in a friendly gathering place."

Born in Calabria, Italy, Leonardo and Alfonso set off in opposite directions to pursue their gastronomic aspirations. Leonardo moved to Tuscany to work with the Luppoli family in the coveted Malborghetto Restaurant, a local "hang-out" for those in the region. This provided the roots of Leonardo's extensive experience for service and quality of authentic cuisine. Meanwhile, the trim and charming Alfonso began his career as a baker in Pietra Paula, Italy. After five years, he joined the Italian military and became the head cook for a division (including top brass), serving in Naples and then Bologna. Leaving the military, Alfonso delved into the produce business in Switzerland, testing new techniques for growing fruits and vegetables.

In 1992, Leonardo made the bold move to the United States where he established the restaurant Pane Caldo in Beverly Hills, California, and worked as a chef at the notable Cicada restaurant in Los Angeles. Eager to

increase his culinary exposure, Leonardo relocated to Aspen, Colorado, and joined the legendary Farfalla Restaurant.

Leonardo's biggest break, and biggest gamble, came in 1997 when he and friend Daniele Serra received a phone call that a restaurant in Central California was up for sale. Deciding to give it shot, the duo purchased the restaurant and renamed it Trattoria Grappolo. Alfonso, who was still living in Italy, heard about the news from his brother, who asked if he would be interested in teaming up. Four days after the restaurant opened, Alfonso relocated to Santa Ynez. The Italian bistro was born.

"We knew the restaurant business was the number one business that fails," says Daniele, who arrives to Grappolo each day on his Italian-made Ducati motorcycle. "But with a little luck, the perfect location, and the right people, we knew we could make it work."

He was right. Today, the casual bistro continues to serve traditional fare from the various regions of Italy to all kinds of customers.

Attractive young singles on dates, families with kids, local ranchers, equestrian moguls, famous vintners, vacationers, Hollywood celebrities—they're all here. In fact, on any given night, dinner guests may find themselves rubbing elbows with Bo Derek, Cheryl Ladd, Kelly LeBrock, Noah Wiley, Ellen DeGeneres or musical icon David Crosby—all regular customers. Without question, Trattoria Grappolo has found the right combination of great food, a family-style atmosphere and impeccable service, and serves it with gusto night in and night out.

"The key is to keep it interesting," says Leonardo, slipping past the crisply attired servers and into the open kitchen. "This makes people come back." But the interesting items aren't all on the menu, extravagant as the menu is. Ordering "off-the-menu" is just one of the Trattoria's secrets that delights devoted guests.

"On a visit to Venice a few years ago, I experienced, for the first time, *Risotto Nero di Seppie* (cuttlefish or squid sautéed in its own indelible ink)," recalls dedicated Grappolo customer Dan Gerber of the famed Gerber baby food

corporation. "Smiling through my blackened teeth and gums, I believed I would not experience this dish again until I returned to Venice. One night at Grappolo, I shared my delightful discovery with Leonardo. 'But Dan,' Leonardo said. 'I can make that for you right now.'"

Of course, one cannot go wrong with sticking to the inviting menu, starting with an order of carpaccio decorated with arugula, Parmesan and extra virgin olive oil, or the restaurant's signature Rollino Veneto—rolled-up pizza pouches stuffed with smoked mozzarella and radicchio.

The evening specials and house-made pastas are also a sure bet, especially the rigatoni with a bevy of mushrooms and the gnocchi in a velvety cream sauce with chicken, pine nuts and rosemary. For meat lovers, the thick New York steak is prepared differently each day, while the rack of lamb is beautifully grilled. Desserts, especially the lavender crème brûlée and the chocolate torte, are worth lingering over. And the expansive wine list proudly features hundreds of bottles of Central California wines from what

Versatility is part of what defines Trattoria. Here is an invitation to sit down
with friends and share food that embodies the generosity of the spirit.

many wine connoisseurs believe to be "wine country at its best."

Outside the expansive windows of Trattoria Grappolo, dining guests can enjoy postcard views of the breathtaking vistas that embrace the restaurant. The Santa Ynez Valley and Los Padres Mountains are studded with ancient oaks, brilliant wild flowers and magnificent vineyards. Although Santa Ynez is a rural, ranching town, it happens to be situated in one of the top wine regions of the world.

The nearby beaches are backed by an unusual mountain configuration with an east-west orientation forming valleys that open directly to the Pacific Ocean. This unique topography allows the inland fog and ocean breezes to shape one of the coolest winegrowing regions in California and create an ideal environment for the cultivation of classic grape varietals. The growing season in Central California is considerably longer than other growing areas, meaning the fruit has an unusually long "hang time" on the vine. This makes for world-class wines of distinctive character—and such superior wines can always be found inside Trattoria Grappolo's award-winning wine cellar.

Like the highly touted Central California wine region, the forecast for Tratorria Grappolo has never looked brighter. It is the perfect setting for lunch, dinner, private parties and corporate get togethers. The Curti brothers also host a variety of cooking classes at neighboring wineries, and offer a full catering service for those seeking a true Italian experience outside the restaurant.

But how do the Curti brothers find kitchen help so they can keep bringing the magic of Italy to the rolling golden hills of Santa Ynez? Easy. Leonardo and Alfonso recently imported their younger brother, Giorgio, from Italy. Then there are Leonardo's twin girls Sophia and Isabella and daughter Camilla, and Alfonso's sons, Giacomo and Luciano. It appears there won't be any shortage of Curti-chefs anytime soon. And that's good news for the Trattoria regulars—and everyone else in the Santa Ynez Valley—who loves traditional Italian food served with the heart and friendly atmosphere of the Old Country.

Our high expectations for quality never exceed

the perfection of the **ultimate purveyor**, nature.

# FRESH ANTIPASTI, SALADS & SOUPS I

IMAGINATION, SIMPLICITY & INFUSION

The beginning courses at Trattoria Grappolo are a blend of imagination, simplicity and the infusion of the rustic regions found throughout Italy. Such exquisite combinations prepared by Chefs Leonardo and Alfonso Curti and their highly trained culinary staff take on the form of colorful antipasto platters, crisp hearty salads and rich decadent soups—all perfected from scratch at the bustling bistro.

As a fine bottle of California wine is uncorked at your table, you will discover all of the bistro's

delectable dishes not only pair well but are simple, easy-to-make dishes designed to please the palate and tantalize your taste buds for what is in store.

Chef Leonardo Curti's rendition of the classic Carpaccio di Manzo whets the appetite as does his garden-fresh Caprese and the Crostino alla Romana, which Chef Curti considers to be his American ham and cheese but with Italian ingredients.

The Insalata di Pollo—crispy free-range chicken, romaine lettuce and Gorgonzola cheese tossed in a creamy Caesar dressing—is another local favorite bursting with a cornucopia of flavors. Craving a salad that unites fresh local ingredients from Central California with exceptional products from Italy? Try the Insalata dell'Ortolana—handpicked field greens tossed in an aged balsamic vinegar dressing accompanied by roasted Italian peppers, eggplant, goat cheese and walnuts.

Like the starter courses served at Trattoria Grappolo, the weather outside the Grappolo doors is radiant and welcoming—bluebird skies and long sunny days with rarely a cloud in sight. It doesn't get very cold in the Santa Ynez Valley, but when it does, the townsfolk scurry indoors. Curling up to a crackling fire with a steaming bowl of Grappolo's signature soups always seem to be the ticket to instant warmth. The next time the elements wreak havoc, try a bowl of Zuppa di Fava or a hearty cup of Zuppa di Lentiche.

# ROLLINO VENETO with TOMATO-BASIL SALAD
*pizza rolls from venice*

**SERVES 8**

1 package active dry yeast

1 cup warm water

2½ to 3 cups all-purpose flour

2 teaspoons salt

1 onion, peeled and thinly sliced

3 tablespoons extra virgin olive oil, divided

1 head radicchio, rinsed, cored and thinly sliced

¾ cup Sangiovese, or other dry red wine

Salt and pepper to taste

8 ounces smoked mozzarella cheese, grated

6 cups diced firm-ripe tomatoes

1 cup slivered basil leaves

2 tablespoons minced garlic

TO MAKE THE DOUGH, in a large bowl, sprinkle yeast over warm water. Let stand until yeast is softened, about 5 minutes. Add 2½ cups flour and salt; beat with a mixer on low speed until incorporated, then on medium-high speed until dough is stretchy, about 3 minutes.

DIVIDE DOUGH IN HALF and shape each half into a ball. Set balls on a lightly floured surface in a warm place and cover loosely with plastic wrap. Let rise until doubled in size, 45 minutes to 1 hour.

MEANWHILE, MAKE THE FILLING in a 10- to 12-inch frying pan over medium-high heat. Stir onion in 1 tablespoon olive oil until limp and beginning to brown, 3 to 5 minutes. Add radicchio and stir often until limp and beginning to brown, 5 to 7 minutes. Stir in wine and cook, stirring occasionally, until evaporated, 10 to 12 minutes. Add salt and pepper to taste and then let cool at least 20 minutes.

PUNCH EACH BALL OF DOUGH down and knead lightly to expel air. On a lightly floured surface, with a lightly floured rolling pin, roll each ball into a 10- to 11-inch round. Sprinkle half the mozzarella over half of each round to within 1 inch of edge; top cheese equally with radicchio mixture. Fold the bare half of each dough round over filling, aligning edges; pinch together to seal. Starting at fold, roll each pizza into a tight log; pinch log ends together to seal. Transfer logs, seam down, to a

*continued on page 30*

12 x 15-inch baking sheet, shaping into equal-size half-rings and spacing at least 3 inches apart. Bake at 425 degrees F in a regular or convection oven until golden brown, 25 to 30 minutes.

MEANWHILE, MAKE THE SALAD. In a bowl, mix tomatoes, basil, garlic and remaining 2 tablespoons olive oil; add salt and pepper to taste.

WITH TWO WIDE SPATULAS, transfer each half-ring to a rimmed board or platter, fitting ends together to form a complete ring. Using a slotted spoon, mound about 2 cups tomato-basil salad in the center of the ring; set bowl with the remaining salad alongside the board or platter. Cut the pizza ring into 1$^1$/$_2$- to 2-inch sections and serve with salad.

## WINE SUGGESTION

*EOS Zinfandel, Paso Robles California.* Zinfandel, like Petite Sirah, is considered an American heritage grape. One reason Zinfandel works so well in Paso Robles is the long, warm growing season, allowing for concentrated fruit and higher brix than other growing areas. The Zinfandel releases are well-balanced and approachable, highlighting the true jammy flavors of the varietal, and the fennel spice of the terroir.

# INSALATA DI POLLO

*crispy chicken, romaine lettuce and gorgonzola cheese in a caesar dressing*

**SERVES 4–6**

1 small bunch rosemary
1 small bunch fresh sage
½ lemon, zested
½ orange, zested
3 cloves garlic, minced
Salt and pepper to taste
2 tablespoons olive oil
12 chicken tender fillets
Flour
2 heads romaine lettuce
Crumbled Gorgonzola
Grated fresh Parmesan cheese

**CAESAR DRESSING**

⅓ cup fresh lemon juice
2 eggs, lightly beaten
1 cup olive oil
2 cloves garlic, crushed
½ teaspoon salt
¼ teaspoon black pepper
¼ teaspoon Dijon mustard
¾ cup grated fresh Parmesan cheese
1 dash Worcestershire sauce
1 tablespoon anchovy paste, or 4 canned anchovy fillets

IN A BOWL, combine the rosemary, sage, lemon and orange zests, garlic, salt and pepper. Add olive oil and mix well. Add the chicken tender fillets and marinate for at least 2 hours in the refrigerator.

MEANWHILE, prepare the dressing by pouring lemon juice and beaten eggs in a blender. Add the olive oil, garlic, salt, pepper, mustard and Parmesan cheese; blend well. Add the Worcestershire sauce and anchovy paste (to taste). Blend all ingredients together and reserve in refrigerator until serving.

TO COOK, remove chicken from marinade and dust with flour. Add the fillets to a hot-oiled skillet over medium-high heat. Cook until chicken is moist and tender and the crust is golden-brown. Remove from heat and set aside. For the salad, wash the romaine and tear into 1-inch pieces. Mound a handful of romaine on each serving dish, add 3 or 4 pieces of chicken and drizzle the chilled dressing over the chicken and lettuce. Top with Gorgonzola and Parmesan cheeses.

## WINE SUGGESTION

*Rancho Sisquoc Winery Chardonnay, Santa María.* Santa Maria's climate and soil is often compared with the renowned growing regions of Sonoma and Napa. The winery's award-winning Chardonnay has a sweet oak, honeysuckle, citrus to melon on the nose with a fabulous buttery mouth-feel. Aged in French Oak, which does not overpower the fruit flavors. The finish is long and balanced.

# Fiori di Zucca Ripieni

*stuffed zucchini blossoms*

**SERVES 4**

1 cup ricotta cheese

½ cup grated or shaved Parmesan cheese

2 cloves garlic, minced

1 tablespoon chopped Italian parsley

1 egg

4 slices salami Toscano, chopped

Pinch of salt

Pinch of nutmeg

8 zucchini blossoms, pistons removed

2 cups olive oil, for frying

**BATTER**

⅓ cup flour

1 egg

1 cup beer

Salt and pepper to taste

IN A LARGE BOWL, mix together the ricotta cheese, Parmesan cheese, garlic, parsley, egg, salami, salt and nutmeg. After the filling is thoroughly mixed, spoon it into a pastry bag for piping. Fill each zucchini blossom with the mixture. Once all the blossoms have been filled, mix the batter in another bowl by combining flour, egg, beer, salt and pepper. When the oil is hot enough for frying, dip each zucchini blossom into the batter and then fry. Turn zucchini blossoms occasionally to achieve an even golden-brown color on all sides. Serve immediately. To serve, plate 2 blossoms per serving and top with grated Parmesan cheese.

## WINE SUGGESTION

*Carina Cellars Clairvoyant.* The goal at Carina Cellars is simple: to produce top-quality Santa Barbara County Rhône wines that showcase and emphasize terroir above all else. In their own words, tasting Clairvoyant is like a hand-in-hand stroll through fields of strawberries and boysenberries leading to the last first kiss—as deep and rich as blackberries and cocoa—followed by violets, sprigs of sage, toffee, cola and white pepper.

# Insalata dell'Ortolano

*mixed greens with eggplant, roasted peppers, walnuts and balsamic vinaigrette*

**SERVES 4**

2 roasted red bell peppers, cut lengthwise into 4 pieces

2 roasted yellow bell peppers, cut lengthwise into 4 pieces

2 Japanese eggplants, cut lengthwise into 4 pieces

3 cups fresh field greens, preferably mixed

4 ounces goat cheese

4 tablespoons ground walnuts

**BALSAMIC VINAIGRETTE**

½ cup extra virgin olive oil

½ cup balsamic vinegar

1 clove garlic, crushed

1 teaspoon Dijon mustard

Salt and pepper to taste

ROAST THE PEPPERS and eggplant under the broiler or on an outdoor grill. Meanwhile, divide the field greens on four plates.

TO PREPARE THE DRESSING, whisk together the olive oil, balsamic vinegar, garlic and mustard in a small bowl. Season to taste with salt and pepper. When vegetables are finished grilling, remove and place on top of the field greens, along with the goat cheese and walnuts. Drizzle the vinaigrette over the salad and serve.

## WINE SUGGESTION

*Mandolina Malvasia Bianca.* This varietal, uncommon to California, is a native of Tuscany and Umbria where it is normally fermented to produce light sweet wine. This wine has been fermented to dryness to showcase another side of Malvasia's personality, intense flowery and spicy aromatics and taste.

# ZUPPA DI LENTICCHIE

*lentil and sausage soup*

**SERVES 4**

¼ cup extra virgin olive oil

¼ cup diced onion

¼ cup diced celery

¼ cup diced carrots

1 clove garlic, smashed

2 to 3 Italian sausages, out of casing and broken into pieces

1 pound lentils

6 to 8 cups water or chicken stock

1 cup diced potato

1 small bunch fresh cilantro, roughly chopped

IN A STOCKPOT, add the olive oil and heat on high. Add the onion, celery, carrots, garlic and sausage. Stir until vegetables are lightly golden, approximately 2 minutes. Add the lentils and 6 cups water or chicken stock. Bring to a boil and then reduce heat to medium. Cook for another 45 minutes to 1 hour. Add remaining 2 cups water or stock as needed. Add potato and continue to cook for another 10 minutes. Add cilantro just before serving.

### WINE SUGGESTION

*Paraiso Vineyards Pinot Noir, Santa Lucia Highlands.* Traditional small-lot fermentations, gentle handling and classic French Oak aging create the look-to-standard for Central Coast Pinot. Pure Paraiso expression: rich cherry and plum flavors, velvety mouth-feel, and balancing, bright acidity.

# Calamari e Fagioli all'Uccelletto
*calamari and bean stew*

**SERVES 4**

4 tablespoons extra virgin olive oil

4 cloves garlic

1 pound calamari rings and tentacles, cleaned

Salt and pepper to taste

8 sage leaves

Pinch of crushed red pepper

¼ cup white wine

2 cans (15 ounces each) cannellini beans, 1 drained and 1 with juice

IN A SAUTÉ PAN over high heat, add the olive oil and garlic and cook until the garlic is slightly golden. Add the calamari, salt, pepper, sage and crushed red pepper. Stir and cook for about 1 minute. Add the wine and let evaporate. Add the beans and continue to cook for about 10 minutes. Divide into bowls and serve immediately with toasted crostino.

## WINE SUGGESTION

*Eberle Winery Mill Road Viognier.* A classic floral bouquet of litchi, honeysuckle and apricot complement mouthwatering flavors of melon and peach and hints of candied ginger culminating in a long, dry finish. An elegant afternoon wine to enjoy by the glass but the rich, full-bodied characteristics of the wine are an ideal companion to enhance seafood or creamy pasta dishes.

# LAMETTE DI SALMONE CON CAPPERI E RUCOLA

*salmon carpaccio with capers and arugula*

**SERVES 4**

2 pounds fresh salmon, thinly sliced

1 cup fresh lemon juice

4 tablespoons capers

Salt and pepper to taste

4 tablespoons extra virgin olive oil

½ pound arugula

SLICE THE SALMON paper thin and let rest in a dish with the lemon juice; refrigerate over night. When ready to serve, drain all the liquid from the dish and place salmon slices on a serving platter. Sprinkle with capers, salt, pepper, olive oil and top with arugula.

**WINE SUGGESTION**

*Rutherford Grove Estate Sauvignon Blanc, Napa Valley.* Aromas and flavors of grapefruit, lemon and guava. From entry to finish a wine of varietal character as expressed from the Rutherford Bench. Ripeness, intensity and acidity are all well balanced with mineral and herbal backnotes.

# CARPACCIO DI BUE

*thinly sliced beef*

**SERVES 4**

4 (3-ounce) medallions beef tenderloin

Sea salt and pepper to taste

4 tablespoons extra virgin olive oil

2 tablespoons capers

½ pound fresh arugula

16 slices fresh Parmesan cheese

2 lemons, halved

LINE KITCHEN COUNTER with plastic wrap, approximately 2 feet long. Place 1 of the beef medallions in the center of the plastic. Place another sheet of plastic wrap on top of the medallion. Using a kitchen mallet, pound fillet evenly until approximately 10 inches in diameter. Uncover plastic wrap and place a dinner plate face down on top of the pounded fillet. Flip plate over with the bottom plastic wrap, which will allow the pounded medallion to be in the center of the plate. Repeat above steps with remaining fillets.

ON EACH PLATED CARPACCIO, sprinkle salt and pepper to taste, drizzle 1 tablespoon olive oil, add ¹/₂ tablespoon capers, and place a small handful of arugula in the center of the carpaccio. Finish with 4 slices Parmesan cheese on top of the arugula and serve with a side of lemon.

## WINE SUGGESTION

*Arbios Wine Cellar Cabernet Sauvignon, Alexander Valley.* Arbios Cellars focuses on a single Bordeaux-style red wine, made from 100 percent Cabernet Sauvignon grapes grown on a mountain top vineyard in the Alexander Valley of Sonoma County. An earthy aroma is accented with scents of cedar, violets and sage. Bright flavors of Bing cherries and rich, warm vanilla. Full-bodied, smooth and balanced.

# CALAMARI ALLA POSITANO

*calamari stuffed with smoked mozzarella and prosciutto*

**SERVES 4**

1 pound fresh calamari tubes
with tentacles

½ cup grated smoked mozzarella cheese

2 tablespoons grated Parmesan cheese

1 teaspoon dry oregano

1 clove garlic, minced

2 tablespoons chopped Italian parsley

2 slices prosciutto

Olive oil

1 cup cherry tomatoes, halved

2 basil leaves, chopped

Salt and pepper to taste

¼ cup extra virgin olive oil

1 head romaine lettuce, to garnish

1 lemon

WASH AND CLEAN CALAMARI, and separate tubes from the tentacles; set aside in a colander to drain. In a blender or Cuisinart, pulse mozzarella, Parmesan, oregano, garlic, parsley and prosciutto until combined. Place mixture into a piping bag and then fill the calamari tubes. With a toothpick, attach the tentacles to the bottom of the tube hole and close the opening. Lightly brush calamari with olive oil. Bring a nonstick pan to high heat and add the calamari. Cook on each side for approximately 2 minutes. Meanwhile, halve and toss the tomatoes in a small bowl with basil, salt, pepper and olive oil. To plate, arrange the lettuce leaves (green), stuffed calamari (white) and cherry tomatoes (red) in order of the Italian flag. Serve immediately with a wedge of lemon.

## WINE SUGGESTION

*Monticello Vineyards Estate Grown Chardonnay.* Monticello Vineyards designated Chardonnays are great examples of how the different clone, rootstock and soil combination specifics in their vineyard combine to create a most harmonious wine. This varietal offers bright complex aromatics featuring pears, peaches and apricots. The blend is focused primarily around fruit, carrying the pear and peach flavors across the palate, ending with a rich finish.

# CROSTINO ALLA ROMANA

*toasted bread with mozzarella, prosciutto and sage*

**SERVES 4**

4 slices country rustic bread (preferably Ciabatta), sliced 1 to 1½ inches thick

1 ball fresh buffalo mozzarella, drained and cut into ½-inch-thick slices

4 tablespoons unsalted butter

15 fresh sage leaves

4 slices prosciutto

PREHEAT BROILER ON HIGH (500 degrees F). Place slices of bread on a baking sheet. Top each slice of bread with the sliced mozzarella. Place baking sheet in oven on the middle rack for approximately 2 minutes, or until mozzarella begins to melt. Meanwhile, in a skillet, melt the butter and add the sage leaves. After mozzarella has melted, remove baking sheet from the oven and top bread slices each with a slice of prosciutto. Place a bread slice on each serving plate and finish by drizzling the butter and sage leaves over top.

## WINE SUGGESTION

*Wildhurst Vineyards Chardonnay, Lake County.* This is a classic Chardonnay style with recognizable Wildhurst touch—advocates on sustainable farming practices. Expect rich and creaminess with toasty oak. Soft acidity allows good focus on the green apple and lemon-lime fruit characters. The creaminess frames flavors of vanilla, toasty caramel and nutmeg.

# ZUPPA DI FAVE

*fava bean soup*

### SERVES 4

4 tablespoons extra virgin olive oil

½ onion, sliced

1 clove garlic, sliced

1 pound fava beans, frozen or dried

4 to 6 cups chicken stock

1 tablespoon fennel seeds

Salt and pepper to taste

4 ounces dry salted ricotta cheese

Truffle oil (as needed)

4 slices country bread, to serve
with the soup

IN A LARGE STOCKPOT over medium heat, add olive oil, onion and garlic and cook for about 5 mintues. Stir in fava beans and cook for another 3 minutes. Add the chicken stock, fennel seeds, salt and pepper. Let cook for about 30 minutes, stirring occasionally. Remove 1 cup of fava bean mixture and purée. Add back to soup. Mix well and serve in individual soup bowls topped with dry salted ricotta cheese, a drizzle of truffle oil, and accompanied by slices of country bread.

### WINE SUGGESTION

*DeLoach Vineyards Chardonnay, Russian River Valley.* This Chardonnay is a blend of premium vineyards located within three miles of the winery in the heart of the Russian River Valley. Carefully tended vines yield fruit of exemplary quality. Ambrosial scents greet you from the glass followed by aromas and flavors of toasted hazelnuts, citrus blossom, guava, papaya and Gravenstein apples.

# ZUPPA DI ZUCCA AL FORMAGGIO

*butternut squash soup with gorgonzola*

**SERVES 4**

2 tablespoons unsalted butter

1 cup diced butternut squash, peeled and cleaned

1 cup water

Salt to taste

1 cup cream

Pepper to taste

4 ounces mild Gorgonzola cheese

IN A LARGE STOCKPOT, melt the butter and add squash over medium heat. Cook for about 5 minutes. Add water and salt and continue to cook for about 20 minutes. Remove squash from heat and purée in a blender. Return the blended squash to the stockpot. Add cream and pepper and bring to a boil. Serve with melted cheese on top.

**WINE SUGGESTION**

*Lucas & Lewellen Sauvignon Blanc, Santa Barbara County.* This Sauvignon Blanc is entirely cold fermented and exhibits the lovely, ripe pear and Golden Delicious apple aromas and flavors for which Lucas & Lewellen is renowned. After fermentation, the wine is racked to new French Oak barrels for three months to gain additional notes of toast, roasted grain and alluring spiciness.

# Melanzane alla Parmigiana

*baked eggplant with tomato, basil and parmesan*

**SERVES 4**

2 whole eggplants, peeled and sliced into
½-inch-thick slices

1 tablespoon salt

Pinch of sugar

4 cups olive oil, for frying

1 cup flour

4 cups Tomato Sauce (see page 92)

1 cup grated fresh Parmesan cheese

6 basil leaves

PREHEAT OVEN TO 375 DEGREES F. Place eggplant in a colander and sprinkle with salt and sugar. Set a plate on top of eggplant, allowing the extra moisture to drip out of colander. Add the oil to a pan over high heat and dust each slice of eggplant with flour. Add the slices to the pan and then fry eggplant until golden-brown on each side; set aside. At this point, you have the option of making individual eggplant Parmesan in ramekins or one large entrée in a 9 x 12-inch casserole dish.

NEXT, LAYER THE BOTTOM of the dish with slices of fried eggplant and lightly top with Fresh Tomato Sauce. Sprinkle with Parmesan cheese and fresh basil leaves. Repeat the same layer process. Bake for about 25 minutes, or until cheese on top is golden-brown.

## WINE SUGGESTION

*Foxen Winery & Vineyard Sangiovese Volpino.* Foxen's Sangiovese Volpino (meaning "little fox") is an extraordinarily food-friendly wine that goes great with a wide array of foods—from tomato-based dishes to steak. This varietal (75% Sangiovese and 25% Merlot) provides excellent acidity and tannins for an extremely well-structured Cal-Ital—style wine. Aromas of cherries and strawberries are beautifully balanced by the soft yet rich mid-palate flavors and texture.

# INSALATA DI TARTUFATA
*truffle salad*

**SERVES 4**

2 heads romaine lettuce

2 heads Belgian endive

1 large potato

2 cups olive oil, to fry

Salt

½ cup crumbled Gorgonzola cheese

**TRUFFLE DRESSING**

2 tablespoons truffle oil

4 tablespoons extra virgin olive oil

½ tablespoon minced shallots

1 tablespoon Dijon mustard

1 tablespoon rice vinegar

Salt and pepper to taste

CUT ROMAINE AND BELGIAN ENDIVE into 1-inch pieces; reserve in refrigerator. Wash and clean the potato. Using a vegetable peeler, make thin-sliced ribbons of potato. Next, heat olive oil in a sauté pan over high heat. When ready, add the potato ribbons and fry until golden-brown on all sides; drain and set aside. Sprinkle with salt and reserve.

WHISK ALL THE DRESSING ingredients together until well incorporated and then assemble the salad by tossing the lettuce with the dressing. Serve on individual salad plates and top with the potato ribbons and Gorgonzola cheese.

## WINE SUGGESTION

*Foppiano Vineyards Petite Sirah, Russian River Valley.* Foppiano's estate-grown Petite Sirah, situated in Sonoma County's Russian River Valley, is their hallmark varietal. This outstanding red wine offers huge structure with deep rich purple color, complex aromas of spices and black pepper, and concentrated flavors of ripe berries and chocolate from the inviting nose to a rich silky finish.

# CAPONATA CON BURRATA

*sweet and sour vegetables with creamy burrata*

**SERVES 4**

1 eggplant, cut into 1-inch pieces

1 cup olive oil, for frying eggplant

¼ cup extra virgin olive oil

1 onion, cut into 1-inch pieces

1 clove garlic, minced

2 stalks celery, cut into 1-inch pieces

1 cup tomato, cut into 1-inch pieces

Salt and pepper to taste

2 tablespoons pine nuts

2 tablespoons golden raisins

1 tablespoon oregano

10 whole green olives, pitted

4 basil leaves

4 tablespoons white wine vinegar

4 tablespoons sugar

4 (3 to 4 ounces each) Burratta cheese or fresh mozzarella

FRY CHOPPED EGGPLANT in olive oil until golden brown; drain and set aside. In a sauté pan, add extra virgin olive oil over medium-high heat. Add onion, garlic and celery. Stir constantly for about 5 minutes, or until vegetables are soft. Add tomato, salt and pepper, pine nuts, raisins and oregano and then lower heat to medium. Cook for about 20 minutes, or until tomatoes are absorbed; set aside to cool. When cool, add eggplant, olives and basil leaves. In a small bowl, add the vinegar and sugar and stir until sugar is dissolved. Slowly add this to the vegetable mixture and taste as you go until desired flavor is reached. Let cool and serve surrounding the Burrata.

## WINE SUGGESTION

*VJB Cellars.* With vintages named in the top 12 by the Wall Street Journal, VJB and their superior vines produce such memorable wines as their Mendocino Barbera. Raspberry, strawberry and cherry flavors abound while its inky black color and incredible depth of flavor give way to refined tannins and a very smooth palatable finish.

# Tortino di Granchio

*italian crab cake with roasted bell pepper sauce*

**SERVES 4–6**

1 pound fresh lump crabmeat

1 egg, whole

3 ounces fresh Parmesan cheese, grated

1 clove garlic, minced

2 tablespoons sour cream

½ tablespoon chopped Italian parsley

Salt and pepper to taste

1 cup flour

½ cup olive oil, to fry

**ROASTED BELL PEPPER SAUCE**

2 red bell peppers, roasted and chopped

½ cup sliced onion

1½ cups cream

Salt and pepper to taste

2 basil leaves, chopped

**TO MAKE THE CRAB CAKES**, mix all ingredients together in a large bowl, except flour and oil. Roll individual crab cakes into a flattened ball so they weigh about 3 ounces each. Dust each cake with flour and fry in a sauté pan with the olive oil over medium heat until golden-brown on both sides. Serve immediately with the Roasted Bell Pepper Sauce.

**FOR THE SAUCE**, sauté the roasted bell peppers and onion in a saucepan for about 4 minutes over medium heat. Add the cream, salt, pepper and basil leaves and continue to cook for an additional 5 minutes. Remove from heat and pour into a blender; purée and strain. Spoon the sauce on the side of each crab cake.

**WINE SUGGESTION**

*Trentadue Winery Sauvignon Blanc, Dry Creek Valley.* This wine is made from grapes grown on the border between Russian River and Dry Creek Valleys. No oak barrels are used during the aging of the wine in order to preserve the wonderful fresh aromas and flavors of citrus, melons, apples and figs typical for this variety. The varietal is handcrafted with 6% Viognier.

# COPPETTE DI PESCE ALLA SAN PIETRO

*tropical seafood salad*

**SERVES 4**

½ pound fresh halibut

½ pound fresh salmon

1 cup lemon juice

1 mango, diced

1 cup diced papaya

1 green onion, diced

1 bunch cilantro, chopped, reserve some sprigs for garnish

¼ cup chopped tomato

1 small cucumber, seeded and chopped

Salt and pepper to taste

2 lemons or limes, cut into wedges

CUT HALIBUT AND SALMON into small pieces and place in a bowl. Add lemon juice to the fish and set in refrigerator for about 4 hours. Meanwhile, dice mango, papaya, green onion; roughly chop cilantro, tomato and seeded cucumber. Place ingredients in a bowl and set in refrigerator. After the fish has been refrigerated, remove, drain and add to the vegetable mixture. Mix well and add salt and pepper to taste. Serve in a martini glass with a wedge of lemon or lime and a sprig of cilantro on top.

## WINE SUGGESTION

*Mauritson Family Winery Dry Creek Valley Sauvignon Blanc.* Truly a wine with a sense of place. Bright pink grapefruit aromas are accented by dried apricot and fresh cut hay. The round texture in the mouth conjures flavors of honeydew melon and peach orchards. The lush yet vibrant mouth-feel gives way to clean balanced acidity in the back of the palate where the wine finishes clean with a hint of mineral.

# INSALATA DI POLIPO

*octopus salad*

**SERVES 4**

1 bay leaf

4 lemons, halved

6 whole peppercorns

2 pounds fresh raw octopus*

1 stalk celery

1 potato, diced and boiled

Salt and pepper to taste

4 tablespoons extra virgin olive oil

2 tablespoons white wine vinegar

2 tablespoons chopped Italian parsley

*If raw octopus is not available, cooked octopus can be used. Cooked octopus will need to be re-cooked to become tender.

IN A LARGE STOCKPOT, add 1 gallon of water, the bay leaf, 2 lemons (4 lemon halves), peppercorns and octopus and bring to a boil. Cook for about 1 hour (20 minutes for cooked octopus), then set pot aside and let cool. Remove octopus and cut into $^1/_2$-inch pieces. In a bowl, add celery, potato, salt, pepper, olive oil, white wine vinegar, juice of the remaining lemons, parsley and mix well. Add the octopus and chill for approximately 1 hour; serve chilled.

**WINE SUGGESTION**

*Chappellet Winery Chenin Blanc.* Bright and lively, bursting with flavors of tropical fruits and citrus, this wine expresses the unique characteristics of the Chenin Blanc varietal. Chappellet preserves the fresh fruit flavors and crisp acidity of this celebrated grape variety by fermenting and aging the wine in stainless steel tanks. Balanced by bright acidity, the wine finishes with a creamy texture.

# ZUPPA DI PESCE

*fresh assortment of seafood in a light tomato broth*

**SERVES 4**

4 tablespoons extra virgin olive oil

4 cloves garlic, smashed

¼ onion, sliced

12 fresh mussels in shell, cleaned

12 manila clams in shell, cleaned

½ pound fresh salmon, divided into 4 pieces

½ pound fresh halibut, divided into 4 pieces

8 fresh shrimp, peeled and deveined

Pinch of salt, pepper, oregano and crushed red pepper

¼ cup white wine

1 cup fresh tomato chunks

16 basil leaves

1 cup clam juice

1 tablespoon chopped fresh Italian parsley

IN A LARGE SAUCEPAN over high heat, add the olive oil, garlic and onion. Add all the seafood except the shrimp. Add salt, pepper, oregano and crushed red pepper and stir. Add the white wine and allow it to evaporate. Add the tomato, basil leaves and clam juice and bring to a boil. Cover pan and continue to cook for about 5 minutes. Add the shrimp and cook several more minutes until the shrimp are red in color, the shellfish have opened (discard any shellfish that have not opened) and the remaining fish is fully cooked. Divide soup into four serving bowls, sprinkle with chopped parsley and serve immediately with a slice of toasted country bread.

## WINE SUGGESTION

*Ironstone Vineyards Chardonnay.* A delightful fragrance of citrus, pears and fresh-cut green apples. The wine's delightfully refreshing crisp mineral style is filled with flavors of mountain-ripe apples, pineapple and butterscotch. Balanced nicely by mild acidity, the finish is crisp and clean.

# VITELLO TONNATO

*thinly sliced veal with tuna sauce*

**SERVES 4–6**

¼ cup olive oil

2 cloves garlic, sliced

1 pound veal tenderloin

2 cups white wine, for glazing

7 ounces tuna, packed in oil

6 anchovy fillets

2 tablespoons capers, plus 1 tablespoon for garnish

2 lemons, 1 squeezed, 1 thinly sliced

1 tablespoon white vinegar

1 cup mayonnaise

Salt and pepper to taste

IN A SAUTÉ PAN large enough to hold the meat, add olive oil over medium-high heat. Stuff the garlic slices into the veal tenderloin by making slits into the meat with a knife tip and inserting the garlic. Add the veal tenderloin to the oil and cook for about 25 to 30 minutes. Glaze with the white wine every 10 minutes. After the meat has cooked thoroughly, remove pan from heat and let cool. Remove the meat from the pan and drain juices into a cup. In a food processor, add $1/2$ cup of the reserved juice, tuna (with the oil), anchovies and capers. Add lemon juice and vinegar and pulse. Add the mayonnaise, salt and pepper and blend together; set aside. Next, slice the veal tenderloin very thin. To serve, arrange the tenderloin slices on a plate. Pour the sauce over the top and finish by garnishing with 1 tablespoon capers and sliced lemon.

## WINE SUGGESTION

*Wild Coyote Estate Winery Syrah.* Wild Coyote, one of the first Paso Robles Syrah producers, handcrafts a very unique 100% Syrah with a blend of Australian and French Clone. It's an elegant wine with a deep opaque and amethyst color. Flavors of jammy plumb, golden syrup, cocoa, toasted almond and wild berries. Round, full-bodied and silky finish. Excellent companion with red meat and seafood.

# House-Baked Breads & Pizzas 2

MOUTH-WATERING, TASTE TENDER

It starts with Trattoria Grappolo's flavorful and trouble-free dough, made fresh daily at the bistro. Once prepared, the dough is crafted into exciting shapes, tastes and textures.

Grappolo's basket of artisan breads and focaccias that accompany every lunch and dinner table is intended to be dipped, dunked and savored. Whether it is swirled into an herbed olive oil, dropped into

a creamy soup or plunged into a spicy spaghetti sauce, baked breads are an integral part of the Italian dining experience at Grappolo.

If you ask Santa Ynez residents, you will quickly learn the bistro's signature bread dish is the Rollino Veneto—rolled pizza dough stuffed with smoked mozzarella and radicchio and baked to a golden brown in the bistro's indoor pizza oven. During plating, fresh Roma tomatoes are diced and spooned in the center with a long drizzle of extra virgin olive oil.

Like the baked breads and Rollino Veneto, Grappolo's brick-oven pizzas are another popular treat and are made to the customer's liking. Although a traditional pizza oven is the preferred cooking method, a conventional oven will work just fine if used with a pizza stone in order to ensure a crisp yet flaky crust.

From Grappolo's delightful Pizza Margherita—homemade tomato sauce, mozzarella cheese and California basil leaves—to the Pizza Salame Toscana—tomato sauce, mozzarella and Tuscan salami—every pizza that departs the Grappolo oven is loaded with aromatics and flavor, and topped with freshly grated Parmesan cheese, a sprinkle of Italian herbs and a drizzle of olive oil—the most common ingredient found in Italian cooking.

# Fresh Baked Focaccia

**MAKES 2 LOAVES**

1 package dry active yeast

1½ cups warm water

½ cup extra virgin olive oil

2 pounds flour

½ tablespoon salt

Sea salt to taste

DISSOLVE THE YEAST in lukewarm water until foamy, then add the olive oil to the mixture. Next, sift flour and salt together into an electric mixer with a dough hook attached. Turn on low speed and add the yeast mixture. Work the dough for about 15 minutes to obtain a smooth and elastic dough. Divide the dough into 2 pieces, and then place them individually into an oiled bowl and cover with plastic wrap; set aside. Allow the dough to double in size. After the dough has risen, remove from bowl and work by stretching the dough into two shallow baking pans and punching it down with fingertips. Sprinkle top with sea salt and olive oil. Allow the dough to rise half of its size. To bake, place pans into a preheated 400 degrees F oven for about 1 hour.

# IMPASTO PER PIZZE

*fresh pizza dough*

**MAKES 6 (10-INCH) PIZZAS**

1 package dry active yeast

2 cups lukewarm water

4 teaspoons sea salt

1½ pounds all-purpose flour

2 tablespoons olive oil

IN AN ELECTRIC MIXER with the dough hook attached, stir yeast and lukewarm water until combined. Add salt and then add flour until dough begins to form and is not sticky, about 10 to 12 minutes.

PLACE DOUGH IN a bowl that has been lightly coated with olive oil. Also coat the entire dough ball. Cover bowl with plastic wrap and let dough rise in a warm place for about 1 hour.

REMOVE DOUGH from bowl and place on a smooth working surface. Divide the dough into 6 balls, about 6 ounces each. Place each dough ball on a lightly floured surface and cover with a towel. Let rise for about 45 minutes.

ONE AT A TIME, roll each dough ball on a floured surface until a thin 10-inch round pizza shape is formed. Store by simply freezing unused dough in plastic wrap.

# Salsa di Pomodoro per Pizza

*homemade pizza sauce*

**MAKES APPROXIMATELY 2 CUPS**

2 cups tomato purée

2 tablespoons extra virgin olive oil

Dash of dried oregano

1 clove garlic, smashed

Salt to taste

IN A BLENDER, add all of the ingredients and purée until combined. Store in refrigerator until ready to use.

# Pane

*fresh baked bread*

**MAKES 2 LOAVES**

2 ounces dry active yeast

2 cups lukewarm water

2 pounds all-purpose flour

½ tablespoon salt

DISSOLVE THE YEAST in half of the lukewarm water and set aside. Allow yeast and water mixture to foam, then add rest of water. Next, sift flour and salt together into an electric mixer with a dough hook attached. Turn on low speed and add the yeast mixture. Work the dough for about 15 minutes to obtain an elasticity.

TRANSFER THE DOUGH to a bowl, cover with a kitchen towel and allow to double in size. Then divide dough in desired amount and to desired shape. Cover again and allow to rise half of its size.

TO BAKE, PREHEAT oven to 375 to 400 degrees F. Bake the bread for 45 minutes to 1 hour on a stone or baking sheet until golden brown.

# Grissini Prosciutto e Salvia

*breadsticks wrapped with prosciutto and
drizzled with butter and sage*

**SERVES 4**

1 (6-ounce) ball Fresh Pizza Dough
(see page 70)

4 slices prosciutto

4 tablespoons butter

12 fresh sage leaves

PREHEAT OVEN TO 375 degrees F. Cut the dough ball into 4 slices.
Stretch and roll each slice into 12-inch-long breadsticks. Bake in the
oven for about 15 to 20 minutes, or until golden brown. Remove from
oven and wrap each breadstick with a slice or two of prosciutto.
Meanwhile, in a saucepan, melt the butter and add sage leaves. To plate,
arrange breadsticks on platter and serve immediately with the melted
butter and sage.

### WINE SUGGESTION

*Suncé Winery Zora's Estate Pinot Noir, Russian River Valley.* The extraordinary
fruits used in this wine were not crushed—their stems were gently
pulled out from beneath them by a special Pinot de-stemmer. Extreme
care was taken to preserve the whole berry character throughout production. The result is a Pinot of tremendous body with bold aromas of
truffles, baked cherries and burnt coffee bean–like essence.

# PIZZA CON SALAME TOSCANO

*pizza with tuscan salami*

**MAKES 1 (10-INCH) PIZZA**

1 (6-ounce) ball Fresh Pizza Dough
(see page 70)

½ cup Homemade Pizza Sauce
(see page 71)

½ cup grated mozzarella

6 to 8 slices Tuscan salami

Extra virgin olive oil

PREHEAT OVEN TO 450 degrees F with a pizza stone inside for 1 hour prior to baking. While oven is preheating, dust a smooth working surface with flour. Place dough ball in center and roll out evenly until about 12 inches in diameter. Spoon pizza sauce evenly over the top and sprinkle generously with the mozzarella cheese. Next, place Tuscan salami slices on top. Using a pizza shovel, place the pizza on the stone and bake for about 10 to 15 minutes, or until crust is golden brown. Remove pizza from oven and drizzle with olive oil.

**WINE SUGGESTION**

*Woodstock Ridge Sangiovese.* The honor of planting and owning a small winery in the Santa Ynez Valley can only be enhanced by pairing Woodstock's fine wines with great food. According to winery owners Jeff Frank and Shawna Parker, the marriage of food and wine is a special and ongoing experience. The Woodstock Ridge Sangiovese is a perfect varietal for this delicious dish.

# Pizza Margherita

*pizza with mozzarella and fresh basil*

**MAKES 1 (10-INCH) PIZZA**

1 (6-ounce) ball Fresh Pizza Dough
(see page 70)

½ cup Homemade Pizza Sauce
(see page 71)

½ cup grated mozzarella

6 to 8 fresh basil leaves

Extra virgin olive oil

PREHEAT OVEN TO 450 degrees F with a pizza stone inside for 1 hour prior to baking. While oven is preheating, dust a smooth working surface with flour. Place dough ball in center and roll out evenly until about 12 inches in diameter. Spoon pizza sauce evenly over the top and sprinkle generously with the mozzarella cheese. Using a pizza shovel, place the pizza on the stone and bake for about 10 to 15 minutes, or until crust is golden brown. Remove pizza from oven and then sprinkle basil leaves on top and drizzle with olive oil.

## WINE SUGGESTION

*J. Wilkes Winery Bien Nacido Vineyards "Hillside" Pinot Noir.* Bien Nacido Vineyards is located on south-facing slopes in the Santa Maria Valley and is recognized as one of the premiere vineyards in California for Pinot Noir grapes. Open a bottle of J. Wilkes' "Hillside" Pinot Noir and enjoy aromas of fresh strawberries, raspberries and currants balanced nicely with smoke and vanilla. On the palate, juicy strawberry and other red fruits are complemented by a silky mouth-feel.

# PIZZA PROSCIUTTO CRUDO E CARCIOFI

*pizza with prosciutto and artichoke*

**MAKES 1 (10-INCH) PIZZA**

1 (6-ounce) ball Fresh Pizza Dough
(see page 70)

½ cup Homemade Pizza Sauce
(see page 71)

½ cup grated mozzarella

6 artichoke quarters, crumbled

4 large slices prosciutto

Extra virgin olive oil

Dried oregano

PREHEAT OVEN TO 450 degrees F with a pizza stone inside for 1 hour prior to baking. While oven is preheating, dust a smooth working surface with flour. Place dough ball in center and roll out evenly until about 12 inches in diameter. Spoon pizza sauce evenly over the top and sprinkle generously with the mozzarella cheese. Add the artichokes and, using a pizza shovel, place the pizza on the stone and bake for about 10 to 15 minutes, or until crust is golden brown. Remove pizza from oven and top with the prosciutto slices. Drizzle pizza with olive oil and a dash of oregano and serve.

**WINE SUGGESTION**

*Trattoria Grappolo's Private Label—Grappolaia, Santa Barbara County.* Produced and bottled by Arthur Earl Winery in the Santa Ynez Valley, the restaurant's Grappolaia is a blend of 67% Cabernet Sauvignon and 33% Sangiovese. Like Grappolaia, Arthur Earl focuses on wines from the grape varieties native to the Rhône Valley of France and Northern Italy as well as a style that produces big, full-bodied, fruit forward red wines.

# Pizza Quattro Formaggi

*pizza with four cheeses*

**MAKES 1 (10-INCH) PIZZA**

1 (6-ounce) ball Fresh Pizza Dough
(see page 70)

½ cup Homemade Pizza Sauce
(see page 71)

¼ cup each grated mozzarella, fontina,
Gorgonzola and hementel cheeses

Extra virgin olive oil, as needed

PREHEAT OVEN TO 450 degrees F with a pizza stone inside for 1 hour prior to baking. While oven is preheating, dust a smooth working surface with flour. Place dough ball in center and roll out evenly until about 12 inches in diameter. Spoon pizza sauce evenly over the top and sprinkle generously with the cheeses. Using a pizza shovel, place the pizza on the stone and bake for about 10 to 15 minutes, or until crust is golden brown. Remove pizza from oven and drizzle with olive oil.

### WINE SUGGESTION

*Paradise Ridge Estate Zinfandel "Hoenselaars Vineyard" Russian River Vineyard.* This small, exceptional vineyard is perfectly positioned on a steep, rocky hillside overlooking Lake Somapecare. The grapes are hand harvested, gently de-stemmed and cold soaked before being transferred into 'open top' tanks where submerged cap fermentation takes place. The vintage includes 8% Petite Sirah and 5% Syrah, making this a complex wine with rich and tempting flavors.

# Pizza con Melanzane alla Parmigiana

*pizza with eggplant parmesan*

**MAKES 1 (10-INCH) PIZZA**

1 (6-ounce) ball Fresh Pizza Dough
(see page 70)

½ cup Homemade Pizza Sauce
(see page 71)

½ cup grated mozzarella

5 slices prepared eggplant (see page 52)

¼ cup grated fresh Parmesan cheese

Extra virgin olive oil

PREHEAT OVEN TO 450 degrees F with a pizza stone inside for 1 hour prior to baking. While oven is preheating, dust a smooth working surface with flour. Place dough ball in center and roll out evenly until about 12 inches in diameter. Spoon pizza sauce evenly over the top and sprinkle generously with the mozzarella cheese. Next, place eggplant slices on top and sprinkle with the Parmesan cheese. Using a pizza shovel, place the pizza on the stone and bake for about 10 to 15 minutes, or until crust is golden brown. Remove pizza from oven and then drizzle with olive oil before serving.

**WINE SUGGESTION**

*Galante Vineyards Red Rose Hill Cabernet Sauvignon, Carmel Valley.* Bright, fresh and lively, Galante Vineyards's Red Rose Hill explodes with the characteristic cherry and berry flavors of California's Carmel Valley vineyards. Delightful upon release, modest tannins provide the character that will allow this wine to age well over the next seven to twelve years.

# HANDCRAFTED PASTAS

3

SIMPLY DELICIOUS, ALWAYS HANDMADE

Whether in for lunch or dinner, guests at Trattoria Grappolo are always guaranteed handmade pastas that are served in a variety of traditional Italian sauces. In fact, the savory sauces that mingle with the fresh pastas are so popular, Chef Leonardo Curti has perfected several of them for bottling and distribution. Crema di Carciofi (an artichoke paste with truffle mousse), Salsa alla Puttanesca (a

tomato-herb based sauce) and Caponata (a vegetable-based sauce with tomato, pine nuts and raisins) are available at grocery stores and markets in the Santa Ynez Valley with national distribution coming soon.

Like his award-winning sauces, Chef Curti and his staff enjoy serving up their personal favorites that combine fresh Central California produce with imported Italian ingredients. Some of the favorites include Spaghetti al Carbonara—fresh pasta lightly tossed with egg, Parmesan cheese and Italian bacon; Spaghetti alla Cipolla—spaghetti sautéed in an onion Parmesan sauce; Tortelloni di Zucca—handmade ravioli filled with pumpkin, ricotta and Parmesan cheese and tossed with butter and sage; and the classic Capellini alla Checca—angel hair pasta served with fresh garden tomatoes, basil, garlic and extra virgin olive oil.

At the famous California bistro, the fettuccine, linguine and rigatoni dishes are simply delicious, always fresh and tossed daily with fresh local ingredients like the shiitake, porcini and champignon mushrooms found in Grappolo's Rigatoni Tre Funghi.

For home cooks who don't have the time to hand make their own pasta, Chef Curti admits today's store-bought pastas are excellent substitutes that work well with his seasoned sauces.

# Pasta Fatta in Casa

*homemade pasta dough*

**SERVES 4**

5 eggs

Pinch of salt

1 tablespoon extra virgin olive oil

3 cups all-purpose flour

IN A SMALL BOWL, beat eggs, salt and olive oil together; set aside. In a food processor or Cuisinart, add the flour and turn on. While processor is operating, slowly add the egg/oil mixture. Stop processing when the dough forms a ball. Remove dough from processor and divide into 3 balls. Wrap each with cellophane and refrigerate at least 20 minutes prior to use. When ready, form or shape pasta dough into desired shape using a pasta maker or by hand.

# Salsa a Pomodoro

*tomato sauce*

**SERVES 4**

¼ cup olive oil

¾ cup sliced white onion

2 cloves garlic, diced

2 (28-ounce) cans Italian peeled tomatoes

3 fresh basil leaves

Salt and pepper to taste

IN A HEAVY SAUCEPAN, pan on medium-high heat, add olive oil, onion, and garlic. Cook until onion turns a light golden yellow, about 3 minutes. Add the tomatoes and bring to a boil. Lower heat and simmer for 20 to 25 minutes. Add basil leaves and work out the chunks of tomatoes with a fork or a whisk. Add salt and pepper to taste and serve over your favorite pasta.

*For Sugo all' Arriabata, a spicy tomato sauce variation, replace onion with 1 teaspoon crushed red pepper and cook in olive oil with 4 cloves crushed garlic (instead of 2 diced) for about 3 minutes. Add 6 basil leaves (instead of 3).*

# INVOLTINI DI MELANZANE

*rolled eggplant with capellini pasta*

**SERVES 4**

**FILLING**

2 cups Tomato Sauce (see page 92)

1 cup ricotta cheese

4 fresh basil leaves

Pinch of salt, pepper and dried oregano

2 pounds capellini pasta


2 large, elongated eggplants

2 cups flour, for dusting eggplants

2 cups olive oil, for frying

12 slices smoked mozzarella cheese

PREHEAT OVEN TO 375 degrees F. In a large bowl, add all the filling ingredients except the capellini and mix well. Meanwhile, cook the capellini according to package directions and drain. Add capellini to the filling and mix well.

THINLY SLICE THE eggplant about $1/8$ inch thick. Dust each slice in flour and fry in olive oil until golden brown. Drain on pan using paper towels. Line the slices of eggplant vertically and place about 1 tablespoon filling in the center of each slice. Roll each eggplant slice and place in a baking dish. Top with slices of smoked mozzarella. Bake for about 10 minutes, or until cheese is golden brown on top. Serve 3 rolls per person.

**WINE SUGGESTION**

*Rideau Vineyard Sangiovese.* Rideau's Sangiovese has perfumed notes of roses, nutmeg and cinnamon that enliven this rich, bold red. A fusion of elegant tannins and brightly flavored fruit result in an immensely enjoyable wine.

# RIGATONI AI TRE FUNGHI

*rigatoni with three-mushroom sauce*

**SERVES 4**

4 tablespoons butter

2 cloves garlic, minced

1 pound fresh sliced mushrooms (porcini, morel, shiitake, champignon or any combination)

$\frac{1}{4}$ cup white wine

Salt and pepper to taste

2 cups Tomato Sauce (see page 92)

1 cup cream

1 pound rigatoni

2 tablespoons white truffle oil

Grated Parmesan cheese, as needed

1 bunch fresh Italian parsley, chopped

IN A SAUCEPAN, melt butter and add garlic over medium-high heat and cook for about 1 minute. Add the mushrooms, wine, salt and pepper. Allow wine to evaporate and add the tomato sauce and cream. Stir well and cook over medium heat for about 10 minutes. Meanwhile, cook the rigatoni according to package directions and drain. Add the pasta to the sauce and mix well. Add the truffle oil, mix again, and serve immediately with fresh Parmesan cheese and Italian parsley.

## WINE SUGGESTION

*Chateau Julien Private Reserve Merlot, Monterey County.* Lush berry and robust dark cherry aromas accented by hints of cedar and vanilla. It's subtle oak age and moderate tannins complement this full-bodied wine's fine acidity and ripe, intense fruit. A nice complexity and texture through a smooth, lingering finish. Racked annually and aged for 29 months in new French Oak barrels.

# MALFATTI

*naked ravioli*

**SERVES 4**

1 cup cooked, chopped and drained spinach

1 cup ricotta cheese

½ cup grated fresh Parmesan cheese

Pinch of ground nutmeg

1 clove garlic, minced

1 egg

Salt and pepper to taste

Italian breadcrumbs (optional)

1 cup flour

IN A LARGE BOWL, mix spinach, ricotta, Parmesan cheese, nutmeg, garlic, egg, salt, pepper, and a handful of breadcrumbs a little at a time if mixture is too wet; mix well. Using a 1-ounce ice cream scoop, scoop the filling into balls. Roll each ball into the flour and coat well. In a large stockpot filled with salted water, bring to a boil. When boiling, add the ravioli balls and cook until they float. Remove the ravioli and serve with melted butter, sage and Parmesan cheese or your favorite sauce.

## WINE SUGGESTION

*Buttonwood Farm Winery & Vineyard Merlot.* Concentrated aromas of plum, cedar and clove give way to flavors of forest floor, cedar, clove, black cherry and oak. A firm backbone of tannin supports the wine without getting in the way of the flavor. The addition of cabernet franc adds structure and a bit of spiciness to the final product.

# Capellini alla Checca

*angel hair pasta with fresh tomato and basil*

**SERVES 4**

1 pound angel hair pasta

4 tablespoons extra virgin olive oil

4 cloves garlic, minced

6 Roma tomatoes, diced

6 fresh basil leaves

¾ cup chicken stock

Pinch of salt and pepper

Grated fresh Parmesan cheese

COOK PASTA ACCORDING to package directions; drain and set aside. In a large skillet, heat olive oil over medium heat and add garlic. Cook for about 1 minute. Add tomatoes, basil, chicken stock, salt and pepper. Cook for 3 minutes and add the cooked pasta. Toss well and serve immediately with Parmesan cheese sprinkled over top.

## WINE SUGGESTION

*Royal Oaks / Roblar Winery Syrah, Santa Ynez Valley.* The winery's Santa Ynez Syrah comes from a small vineyard called Tierra Alta. Located in the heart of the Ballard Corridor, the unique Central California region provides a perfect micro-climate for growing this prized varietal. The Syrah is aged for 24 months in 80% new French Oak. The wine hits the front of the palate with an explosion of fruit, but finishes with a touch of spice.

# RISOTTO AL NERO DI SEPPIE
*black squid ink risotto*

**SERVES 4**

¼ cup olive oil

1 medium onion, finely diced

2 cloves garlic, minced

1 cup squid rings and tentacles, cleaned

Salt and pepper to taste

¼ cup white wine

1 tablespoon squid ink (fresh or bottled)

5 to 6 cups clam juice, chicken stock or water

2 cups risotto

12 shrimp, peeled and deveined

4 tablespoons unsalted butter

1 tablespoon chopped fresh Italian parsley

IN A SAUCEPAN with the olive oil, sauté the onion and garlic for about 5 minutes, or until the onion is soft and golden. Add the squid, salt and pepper. Add the white wine and reduce. Next, add the squid ink and half of the clam juice, chicken stock or water. Add the risotto and bring to a boil. Reduce heat and let simmer for about 25 minutes, adding the remaining liquid a little at a time. About 5 minutes before finishing, add the shrimp and cook until tender. Remove from heat and add the butter and parsley, stirring constantly until creamy. Serve immediately.

## WINE SUGGESTION

*Dry Creek Vineyard Fumé Blanc, Sonoma County.* The winery's Fumé Blanc's quintessential varietal character has made it a benchmark Sauvignon Blanc in California and a flagship at the winery. The wine exhibits romas of citrus, grapefruit, melon and lemongrass. The balanced, crisp acidity cleanses the palate and invites an array of foods, including goat cheese, seafood and fresh oysters.

# Ravioli di Pesce

*fish ravioli*

**SERVES 4**

1 pound fresh sea bass or other white flaky fish

½ cup white wine

½ cup clam juice

4 cups water

1 pound broccoli

4 tablespoons extra virgin olive oil

2 cloves garlic, minced

Pinch of crushed red pepper

2 anchovy fillets

Salt and pepper to taste

Homemade Pasta Dough (see page 92)

Breadcrumbs (optional)

1 egg, beaten

IN A ROASTING PAN, add fish, wine and clam juice and roast until cooked. In a pot, add water and bring to a boil. Add the broccoli and cook for about 4 minutes, drain, remove broccoli and set aside. In a sauté pan, add olive oil, garlic, crushed red pepper and anchovy fillets; cook for about 2 minutes. Add the broccoli, sea bass, salt and pepper; mix well. Transfer all of the ingredients into a Cuisinart and pulse until mixture is fully combined; set aside.

MAKE THE PASTA DOUGH and roll out flat and thin. Cut into large ravioli squares. With a 1-ounce ice cream scoop, scoop fish filling into the center of the pre-cut ravioli squares. (Note: If the filling is too wet, add some Italian breadcrumbs.) With 1 beaten egg, use a pastry brush and dip into the egg wash. Brush both sides of the square ravioli dough and fold one corner to another creating a triangle. Gently press around the filling area to remove any air pockets. Cut the pasta edges with a zigzag cutter to make a half-moon shape. Repeat process until finished with the fish mixture.

MEANWHILE, BRING a large stockpot with water to a boil. After boiling, salt the water and add 4 to 5 raviolis. Cook each batch for about 3 to 4 minutes. Drain each ravioli with a large slotted spoon and serve with Spicy Tomato Sauce (see page 92).

## WINE SUGGESTION

*Sunstone Vineyards & Winery Reserve Chardonnay, Santa Barbara County.* Pristine in clarity, this Chardonnay has a glistening, golden hue. Pear, red and green apple and pineapple carry the bouquet of this wine. The palate expresses nice acidity and confirms the nose with the fruit flavors of passion fruit, pear, apple and pineapple, making for a pleasant and persistent finish.

# Fettuccine al Capriccio
*fettuccine pasta with tomato, artichoke and capers*

**SERVES 4**

¼ cup olive oil

½ onion, thinly sliced

½ pound fresh artichoke hearts

½ cup chopped porcini mushrooms

¼ cup white wine

Salt and pepper to taste

2 cups canned tomatoes, crushed

2 tablespoons capers

4 fresh basil leaves

1 pound egg fettuccine

2 tablespoons white truffle oil

Fresh buffalo mozzarella, diced

IN A LARGE SAUCEPAN, over high heat, add the olive oil and onion. Cook for about 2 to 3 minutes. Add artichoke hearts and continue to cook for several more minutes. Add the mushrooms, wine, salt and pepper. Cook until wine is evaporated. Add tomatoes and bring sauce to a boil; lower heat to simmer. Add capers and basil leaves and continue to simmer for another 10 minutes. Meanwhile, cook the fettuccine in salted water according to package directions and drain. Add cooked pasta to the sauce. Add truffle oil and mix well. Top with buffalo mozzarella. Serve immediately.

## WINE SUGGESTION

*Mosby Winery & Vineyard's Dolcetto.* Mosby Winery and Vineyard are producers of award-winning Cal-Italia wines from estate-grown fruit, including Dolcetto (a grape originating in the Piedmonte region of northern Italy). Although the name means "little sweet one," Dolcetto wines are not sweet. The nose of the Mosby Dolcetto has hints of cranberry, brown spice and forest floor. The clean, dark berry flavors are followed by a firm, spicy finish.

# SPAGHETTI ALLA CARBONARA
*spaghetti with eggs and italian bacon*

**SERVES 4**

4 egg yolks

½ cup cream

¼ cup grated fresh Parmesan cheese

Salt and pepper to taste

¼ cup olive oil

½ pound diced pancetta (Italian bacon)

1 pound spaghetti

IN A BOWL, mix egg yolks, cream, Parmesan cheese, salt and pepper. Meanwhile in a saucepan, bring olive oil to medium heat and add the pancetta. Cook pancetta in saucepan until golden brown and set aside. Next, cook the spaghetti according to package directions and drain. Add the spaghetti to the cooked bacon, mix well and return saucepan to medium-low heat. Pour in egg mixture and fold in with the pasta and bacon. Do not allow curds to form. Top with a generous amount of grated Parmesan cheese and serve immediately.

**WINE SUGGESTION**

*Brander Vineyards Cuvee Natalie.* This cuvee is a very original and unique blend, homage to the French-Alsatian white blends. Starting with a backbone of 55% Sauvignon Blanc, Brander has added 17% Riesling, 14% Pinot Gris and 14% Pinot Blanc. Four different varietals in one very fresh and complex little lady. Enjoy ripe and spicy tropical aromas of pineapple and guava with hints of orange marmalade, lemon curd and melon rind. Extremely refreshing.

# TORTELLONI DI ZUCCA

*tortelloni with pumpkin*

**SERVES 4**

**FILLING**

1 cup canned pumpkin

1 cup ricotta cheese

¼ cup grated Parmesan cheese

1 tablespoon diced Italian mostarda

Dash of ground nutmeg

Salt and pepper to taste

Italian breadcrumbs (optional)

**TORTELLONI**

1 package large wonton skins (or
Homemade Pasta Dough, see page 92)

2 eggs

2 tablespoons butter

5 fresh sage leaves

3 cups cream

Salt and pepper to taste

4 amaretto cookies, crushed and crumbled

IN A LARGE BOWL, mix all the filling ingredients together. If pumpkin mixture is very wet, add breadcrumbs until drier mixture is achieved; set aside.

TO MAKE THE TORTELLONI, place wonton skins or pasta dough on a flat work surface. Using a 1-ounce ice cream scoop, place 1 scoop of pumpkin mixture into the center. In a separate bowl, beat the eggs for an egg wash. Using a pastry brush, dip brush into the egg wash and brush both sides of the skin or dough and fold into a triangle. Gently press around the filling area to remove any air pockets. Brush the two bottom corners of the triangle with the egg wash and pull corners together with one corner on top of the other. Repeat process until finished with the pumpkin mixture.

IN A LARGE SAUCEPAN, add the butter and sage leaves. After butter has melted, add the cream, salt and pepper and then reduce the sauce by one-third. Meanwhile, in a large stockpot with boiling water, add the tortelloni and cook for about 2½ minutes; drain and add to the sauce. Serve immediately with amaretto cookies on top.

**WINE SUGGESTION**

*Foley Estates Vineyard & Winery Pinot Noir.* Located in the Santa Ynez Valley, Foley Estates Vineyard & Winery is planted with over 100 acres of Pinot Noir which are divided into unique micro-blocks. Foley's Pinot Noir is dark crimson in color. Notes of boysenberry, blueberry, blackberry, cherry cola, vanilla and earth exude from the glass. Expect moderate tannins, elegant body, broad and dense mouth-feel and a long lingering finish.

# Pasta con le Sarde

*pasta with sardines*

**SERVES 4**

3 quarts water

1 tablespoon salt

7 ounces fresh fennel tops

6 tablespoons extra virgin olive oil

1 medium onion, finely chopped

2½ tablespoons pine nuts

2 tablespoons seedless white raisins

2 to 3 salted anchovies, rinsed and de-boned

¼ teaspoon saffron, dissolved in 1½ tablespoons hot water

12 ounces sardines, fresh or canned in oil

Salt and pepper to taste

10 ounces bucatini pasta

¼ cup ground pistachios

FILL A LARGE POT with the water and salt; cook the fennel tops in salted water for about 10 to 15 minutes, or until soft. Remove the fennel and finely chop; reserve the water. In a saucepan, add the olive oil and onion and cook over medium-high heat for about 5 minutes; stir frequently. Add the pine nuts, raisins, chopped fennel and anchovies and stir well. Next, add the saffron, sardines, salt and pepper. (Note: If using fresh sardines, allow them to cook thoroughly.) Meanwhile, cook the bucatini in the fennel water according to package directions and drain. Add the bucatini to the sauce and mix well. Serve in bowls topped with the ground pistachios. Serve immediately.

**WINE SUGGESTION**

*Trattoria Grappolo Syrah, Santa Barbara County.* Produced and bottled by William James Cellars in the Santa Ynez Valley, the restaurant's Private Label Syrah is aged in ⅓ new oak barrels. The wine has an awesome color, nice mouth-feel, and is very easy drinking with ripe fruit aromas and flavors.

# PENNE CON FUNGHI SALSICCIA

*penne pasta with mushrooms and sausage*

**SERVES 4**

2 cloves garlic, minced

4 mild Italian sausages, casing removed and crumbled

1 pound champignon mushrooms, sliced

½ cup white wine

2 cups Tomato Sauce (see page 92)

1 cup cream

1 pound penne pasta

2 tablespoons white truffle oil

Pinch of crushed red pepper

Salt and pepper to taste

Grated fresh Parmesan cheese

1 tablespoon chopped Italian parsley

IN A LARGE SAUCEPAN on medium heat, add the garlic and sausage and cook until sausage is cooked throughout. Add the mushrooms and sauté for about 2 minutes. Add the wine and increase the heat to high. Add the tomato sauce and cream and cook for about 5 minutes. Meanwhile, bring a stockpot of salted water to a boil. Add pasta and cook according to the package directions. Drain pasta and add to sauce. Add the truffle oil and crushed red pepper; mix well. Add salt and pepper and then top with Parmesan cheese and Italian parsley. Serve immediately.

## WINE SUGGESTION

*J Vineyards & Winery Pinot Noir, Russian River Valley.* J Vineyard's Pinot Noir exhibits the full potential of the vineyard and unique terroir of the region. Bing cherry and plum aromas burst forth. Hints of blackberry, violets, wild fennel, spicy cinnamon and creamy vanilla round out the bouquet. The finish is full, long and silky with coffee, smoked bacon, warm spice and brown sugar notes.

# SPAGHETTI ALLA CIPOLLA

*spaghetti sauté in onion parmesan sauce*

**SERVES 4**

¼ cup extra virgin olive oil

2 large yellow onions, sliced

½ cup chicken stock

1 pound spaghetti

Salt and pepper to taste

Fresh grated Parmesan cheese

2 tablespoons chopped fresh Italian parsley

IN A SKILLET OR SAUTÉ PAN over medium-high heat, add the olive oil and onions. Stir often so the onions do not burn. Add the chicken stock and cook approximately 10 to 15 minutes, or until onions are soft and starting to golden; reduce heat to low. Meanwhile, boil pasta in salted water according to package directions and drain. Add drained pasta to the onions. Mix well and add salt and pepper. Serve immediately topped with fresh grated Parmesan cheese and Italian parsley.

## WINE SUGGESTION

*Hahn Estates Chardonnay, Monterey County.* Hahn Estates, located in Monterey County, is home to a number of California's highly regarded and innovative appellations. Hahn wines, including their crisp Chardonnay, are created from stunningly beautiful vineyards that are stylistically complex, supple and enjoyable upon release. Experience aromatics of peaches, pineapples and lemon zest followed by stone fruit flavors, finishing with a crisp apple tart.

# MALLOREDDUS

*sardinian gnocchi*

**SERVES 4**

4 tablespoons olive oil

½ cup diced onion

4 mild Italian sausages, casing removed
and crumbled

Pinch of crushed red pepper

¼ cup dry red wine

1 pinch saffron

1 (28-ounce) can tomatoes, puréed

1 pound gnocchi

Grated fresh Parmesan cheese

Fresh Italian parsley, chopped

IN A HEAVY SAUCEPAN, add the oil and onion and cook over medium heat for about 5 minutes. Add the crumbled sausage. Next, add the crushed red pepper, wine and saffron. Add the tomato purée, reduce heat and simmer for about 25 to 30 minutes. Meanwhile, cook the gnocchi in boiling salted water according to package directions. Drain gnocchi and add to the sauce. Mix well and serve immediately. Top with Parmesan cheese and Italian parsley.

**WINE SUGGESTION**

*Castoro Cellars Estate Zinfandel, Cobble Creek.* This wine is from organic-grown grapes in the traditional head-pruned style. These limited production grapes are grown to produce wines of distinction with deep color and flavor extraction. Castoro Cellars notices their vineyard tends to exhibit great raspberry fruit notes, along with elegant fruit and ripe plum aromas coupled with a spiciness characteristic of rich Zinfandels.

# TAGLIOLINI ALLA BOTTARGA

*tagliolini pasta with shrimp, clams and tuna row*

**SERVES 4**

¼ cup extra virgin olive oil

2 cloves garlic, smashed

12 manila clams

½ cup chopped fresh Italian parsley

¼ cup dry white wine

Dash of crushed red pepper

12 shrimp, cleaned

1 pound tagliolini pasta

1 cup cherry tomatoes, halved

2 handfuls fresh arugula

4 ounces bottarga (tuna row), grated

IN A MEDIUM SKILLET, heat olive oil. Add garlic, clams and parsley and cook for about 10 minutes. Add wine, crushed red pepper and shrimp and simmer on low heat for about 5 minutes. Meanwhile, cook tagliolini according to package directions and drain. When shrimp are red in color, add pasta to sauce along with the tomatoes and arugula. Mix well and serve in bowls topped with grated bottarga.

## WINE SUGGESTION

*Flying Goat Cellar's Pinot Noir, Rio Vista Vineyard.* Jewel-like glints of garnet shine through the brilliant clarity of the Rio Vista Pinot Noir. There is a bit of masculinity to this wine and with a swirl, notes of leather, pepper and dark blackberries unfold. A taste confirms the nose, adding smoky, mouth-coating tastes of cola and dried blueberry. A medium body and firm structure are joined by lingering layers of dark fruit, earth and dusty baker's chocolate tannins.

# RISOTTO ALLA CREMA DI SCAMPI

*risotto with scampi*

**SERVES 4**

20 shrimp (tails only)

¼ cup extra virgin olive oil

1 clove garlic, chopped

¼ cup brandy

1 cup tomato purée

¼ cup cream

¼ cup olive oil, for cooking rice

1 shallot, diced

1¼ cups arborio rice

1 cup white wine

4 cups vegetable stock

Salt and pepper to taste

1 tablespoon unsalted butter

2 tablespoons chopped fresh Italian parsley

WASH, PEEL AND REMOVE tails from shrimp if need be. In a sauté pan over medium heat, add the olive oil and garlic and cook until garlic is golden. Add half the shrimp tails and cook for several minutes. Add the brandy and tomato purée and cook 8 additional minutes. Add the cream and cook several minutes more; set the scampi cream sauce aside. In another sauté pan, add olive oil and shallot and cook for 2 to 3 minutes. Add the remaining shrimp tails and rice. Stir for 1 minute. Add the wine and let alcohol evaporate. Add the vegetable stock until rice is covered and then add salt and pepper. Cook for 3 to 4 minutes. Just before rice is done, add the contents from the first sauté pan to the second pan with the shrimp and rice, along with the scampi cream sauce, butter and chopped parsley; stir well. Remove from heat and serve immediately.

**WINE SUGGESTION**

*Kalyra Winery Viognier.* This grape has become one of the new rising stars in California. At Kalyra, winemaker Mike Brown has produced his second vintage of this flavorful wine with fruit sourced from the hillside of the White Hawk vineyards in Los Alamos, California. The wine showcases pear and sweet apricot with a hint of honey on the nose. Unlike some white Rhône varietals it has subtle acidity and body with a delicate fruit finish.

# SPAGHETTI CON SCAMPI CARCIOFI
*spaghetti with shrimp and artichoke pesto*

**SERVES 4**

2 cloves garlic, smashed

1 tablespoon chopped fresh Italian parsley

1 cup artichoke hearts

4 cups grated Parmesan cheese

Salt and pepper to taste

1/4 cup olive oil, divided

16 shrimp, cleaned, peeled and deveined

1/4 cup white wine

1 pound linguini or spaghetti

2 tablespoons white truffle oil

Ricotta salata, shaved for garnish

IN A FOOD PROCESSOR, add the garlic, parsley, artichoke hearts, Parmesan cheese, salt, pepper and half of the olive oil. Pulse until mixed well. Add a little water if mixture is too dry. In a sauté pan, add the remaining olive oil and shrimp and cook over medium-high heat for about 2 minutes. Add the white wine and artichoke pesto; mix well. Meanwhile, cook pasta in boiling salted water according to package directions and drain. Add the cooked pasta to the sauce and then add the truffle oil. Mix well, and serve immediately topped with ricotta salata shavings.

## WINE SUGGESTION

*Robert Hall Winery Sauvignon Blanc, Paso Robles.* This Sauvignon Blanc is produced with a goal of maximizing freshness and preserving varietal flavor. It is vivid straw green in color and features aromas reminiscent of fresh crisp apple, pineapple and herbs with hints of toasted almond wrapped around a solid mineral core. In the mouth, the wine exhibits bright varietal fruit flavors that echo the aromas. It is refreshingly dry, medium-bodied with a balancing crisp acidity.

# Risotto al Ragú di Agnello

*risotto with lamb ragu*

**SERVES 4**

¼ cup olive oil

1 cup each diced onion, celery and carrots

1 clove garlic, minced

1 pound ground lamb

½ cup white wine

1 can (28 ounces) tomato purée

Salt and pepper to taste

1 bay leaf

Chicken stock (optional)

4 sage leaves, chopped fine

2 cups risotto

2 tablespoons truffle oil

1 tablespoon butter

Grated fresh Parmesan cheese

IN A STOCKPOT, add the olive oil, vegetable mix and garlic, and cook over medium heat for about 5 minutes. Add the ground lamb and cook for 10 minutes, or until meat is crumbled. Add the white wine and allow the alcohol to evaporate. Add the tomato purée, salt, pepper and bay leaf. Bring to a boil then reduce heat and simmer for about 1 hour. If the meat sauce appears dry, add chicken stock, a little at a time. Add the sage leaves 10 minutes before cooking is complete. About 5 minutes before cooking is complete, cook the risotto according to package directions. Add the risotto to the lamb ragu and mix well. Add truffle oil and butter and mix again. Serve immediately with Parmesan cheese.

## WINE SUGGESTION

*William James Cellars Pinot Noir, Santa Barbara County.* Fermented in open top one-ton fermentors, this "Ruby Charmer" is aged in 33% French Oak barrels and boasts a delicious new release. Enjoy fruity aromas with a Bing cherry finish. William James Cellars acquires its extraordinary wine grapes from over 80 vineyards on the Central Coast, including Garey Ranch & Casa Torres Vineyards where the acclaimed Pinot grapes are grown.

# Pennette al Pesto con Gorgonzola

*penne pasta with basil pesto and gorgonzola*

**SERVES 4**

**BASIL PESTO**

2 cups packed fresh basil leaves

½ cup extra virgin olive oil

2 tablespoons pine nuts

½ cup grated Parmesan cheese

2 cloves garlic, minced

Salt and pepper to taste

1 pound pasta, preferably spaghetti

1 cup cream

4 ounces mild Gorgonzola cheese

Grated fresh Parmesan cheese

COMBINE ALL THE ingredients for the pesto in a food processor or Cuisinart and pulse until a green loose paste forms; set aside. Bring a large stockpot filled with salted water to a boil. Cook pasta according to package directions. Next, add the cream and Gorgonzola cheese to a saucepan and melt cheese over low heat; set aside. Drain pasta and toss with the cheese sauce and then stir in the pesto. Top with Parmesan cheese and serve immediately.

**WINE SUGGESTION**

*Optima Winery Petite Sirah, Dry Creek Valley.* A dense, ripe, full-flavored rendition of one of Sonoma County's most scarce and special red wine grapes. Its blackberry and blueberry aromas are balanced by rich sweet oak and vanilla. The intense berry fruit is integrated into a lush background of youthful tannins, and the flavors blend together in a rich, broad, mouthfilling finish.

# Entreé Specials & Seafood Delights

RUSTIC ITALIAN CUISINE AT ITS BEST

Chef Leonardo Curti admits coming up with daily specials at Trattoria Grappolo is like taking a culinary voyage through Italy—there are so many fantastic delights that await, you never run short of ideas.

"I create specials that reflect the many regions of Italy while making sure to incorporate fresh California ingredients," says Chef Leonardo Curti. "Our dining guests want to experience both elements when they come in so we always promise to deliver."

From the sliced New York steak fanned on a bed of fresh arugula to the succulent California spiny lobster pulled from the cool waters off the Santa Barbara coast, the combination of rustic Italian cuisine with a Central California flare is what makes Trattoria Grappolo an exotic destination where passports are not required.

Preparing such specials like the Sautéed Veal Chop with Morel Mushrooms and Brandy or Grappolo's most requested seafood dish, Cioppino Italiano—a savory fish and shellfish stew—is easy to do at home, as long as you are open to having fun. Chef Curti compares home cooking to driving in Italy—or anywhere for that matter.

"You are given a set of driving directions to follow, but sometimes it doesn't work out as planned," says the seasoned chef. "Suddenly, you come to an exit closed sign or a one-way street you didn't intend on taking. What do you do? You rely on your driving experience and instinct, which allows you to create the appropriate detours to get you back on track. The same methodology applies to cooking. Say you need to sauté a salmon fillet in white wine and an amount of wine isn't given, or perhaps your pizza dough turns out too sticky. Take a deep breath and relax. Everything will be okay." Chef Curti advises home cooks to think outside the box and rely on their intuition rather than believing a cookbook is a bible. If there isn't enough white wine in the pan, simply add some more. If the pizza dough is too sticky, add a bit more olive oil or flour. By going with the flow and cooking with the "blinders off," home cooks and veteran chefs alike will be able to perfect delicious dishes night in and night out—and do so with a smile.

# TAGLIATA DI MANZO

*sliced new york steak over arugula with shaved parmesan cheese*

**SERVES 4**

4 (10- to 12-ounce) New York steaks

¼ cup extra virgin olive oil

3 cups fresh arugula, divided into 4 portions

½ cup cherry tomatoes, halved

Olive oil

Sea salt and fresh cracked pepper to taste

Parmesan cheese, shaved

2 lemons, cut in wedges for garnish

RUB EACH STEAK with olive oil. Grill the steaks under the broiler or on an outdoor grill until medium-rare (or until your liking) and let rest for 10 minutes. Meanwhile, mound a handful of arugula in the center of each plate, add the tomatoes and drizzle with olive oil. Slice the steak in thin strips and arrange over the arugula. Add sea salt and fresh cracked pepper to taste. Top with Parmesan cheese, drizzle with olive oil once more, and serve immediately with lemon wedges.

**WINE SUGGESTION**

*Flora Springs Winery & Vineyards Poggio del Papa.* Pope Valley, located in Napa Valley, is the last frontier of Napa because of its lack of water and continental influences. At Flora Springs, however, an abundance of water and strong afternoon breezes allow their vines to produce bright, intense fruit. Expect tart cranberry flavors of Sangiovese with cherry and raspberry from the Cabernet and Merlot.

# MEZZO POLLO AL FORNO CON FUNGHI PORCINI E ROSMARINO
*roasted chicken with porcini mushrooms and fresh herbs*

**SERVES 4**

4 chicken halves

Salt and pepper to taste

¼ cup extra virgin olive oil

4 cloves garlic, whole

Small bunch of mixed herbs (rosemary, sage, basil and Italian parsley)

½ cup porcini mushrooms

½ yellow onion, sliced

2 tablespoons truffle oil

3 cups chicken stock

4 tablespoons unsalted butter

PREHEAT OVEN TO 400 degrees F. Rub chicken with salt and pepper, olive oil, garlic and herbs. Place chicken in a roasting pan and roast for about 35 minutes. Remove chicken from oven and add the remaining ingredients to the pan. Place the chicken on top of the ingredients and continue roasting until chicken is moist and tender. Save the pan juice to pour on top of chicken prior to serving.

## WINE SUGGESTION

*St. Supéry Virtú Napa Valley White Wine.* The Sauvignon Blanc and Semillon grapes for this wine were carefully harvested and fermented in predominantly French Oak barrels to maintain the delicate fruit flavors. Upon opening, wonderful aromas of honeysuckle, citrus blossoms and melon show up quickly in the aroma followed by pear and peach on the palate from the Sauvignon Blanc and crème and lemon meringue from the Semillon. This wine ages well.

# FIORENTINA AL PEPE VERDE

*grilled porterhouse with green peppercorn sauce*

**SERVES 4**

4 (16-ounce) porterhouse steaks

Salt and pepper to taste

Olive oil

**GREEN PEPPERCORN SAUCE**

1 tablespoon butter

4 teaspoons green peppercorns

¼ cup brandy

2 cups cream

3 tablespoons Dijon mustard

Salt and white pepper to taste

2 sprigs each rosemary, thyme and sage (tied together)

BRUSH THE STEAKS with salt, pepper and olive oil. Grill the steaks under the broiler or on an outdoor grill until medium-rare (or to your liking). Meanwhile, prepare the Green Peppercorn Sauce. When steaks are finished, remove from heat, plate and serve with the Green Peppercorn Sauce.

FOR THE SAUCE, melt butter in a sauté pan over high heat; add peppercorns and then remove from heat. Add the brandy and allow to evaporate. Return to stove and add the cream, Dijon mustard, salt, white pepper and bouquet of herbs. Stir frequently and allow to simmer, about 5 minutes. Remove from heat and serve over red meat, discarding the herb bouquet.

**WINE SUGGESTION**

*Huber Cellars Estate Dornfelder.* Dornfelder is truly unique. Not only is the Huber Vineyard one of the few places in the United States growing Dornfelder, but it produces an amazing cluster and a truly interesting wine. It is difficult to call this varietal a red wine, as it is almost black in the glass. But expect a wonderful bold and robust wine with earthiness and big, dark fruit surrounded by pleasing acidity and integrated tannins.

# SPINACI SALTATI

*sautéed spinach*

**SERVES 4**

¼ cup olive oil

4 cloves garlic

Pinch of crushed red pepper

2 anchovy fillets

2 pounds fresh, cleaned spinach

Salt and pepper to taste

1 lemon, cut into wedges

IN A LARGE SAUTÉ PAN, add the olive oil and garlic and cook over medium-high heat until garlic is soft and golden. Add the crushed red pepper and anchovy fillets. Add the spinach, salt and pepper and stir well until spinach is wilted. Drain the liquid and serve the spinach with lemon wedges.

# Fagioli con Salsicce all 'Uccelletto

*roasted italian sausage with cannellini beans*

**SERVES 4**

8 mild Italian sausages

3 tablespoons unsalted butter

12 fresh sage leaves

Pinch of crushed red pepper

4 cloves garlic

2 cans (15 ounces each) cannellini beans, with liquid

Salt and pepper to taste

POKE SEVERAL HOLES into the sausage with a fork or knife. Roast sausage at 400 degrees F until the meat is cooked through, about 15 to 20 minutes. While sausage is roasting, melt the butter in a saucepan over medium-high heat and add the sage leaves, crushed red pepper, garlic, beans, salt and pepper; cook until creamy. Keep warm until ready to serve. When sausage is finished, remove from oven and serve with the creamed cannellini beans.

### WINE SUGGESTION

*Zaca Mesa Winery & Vineyards Syrah, Santa Ynez Valley.* Since 1972, Zaca Mesa has been handcrafting wines from grapes grown in their vineyards to express their distinct character and genuine quality, offering wine lovers a unique experience to share. Their estate-bottled Syrah displays rich blackberry, cassis and their signature sage spice aromas and flavors. The finish lingers from the ripe tannins and smoky oak. This full-bodied wine ages well.

# PETTO DI POLLO ALLA SALVIA

*sautéed chicken with milk, sage and garlic*

**SERVES 4**

¼ cup extra virgin olive oil

4 (6- to 8-ounce) boneless, skinless
chicken breasts

1 cup flour, for dusting

4 cloves garlic

12 fresh sage leaves

Salt and pepper to taste

½ cup dry white wine

1 cup milk

IN A SAUTÉ PAN over medium-high heat, add the olive oil. Dust the chicken with flour and place in pan. Cook each side for 3 minutes. Add the garlic, sage, salt and pepper. Continue to cook for 2 minutes. Add the wine and allow alcohol to evaporate. Add the milk and continue to cook until chicken is moist and tender. Plate chicken and top with sauce from pan.

**WINE SUGGESTION**

*Melville Winery Estate Chardonnay.* This varietal is 100% from their Santa Rita Hills estate. The fruit is harvested by hand then gently whole-cluster pressed, cold settled overnight and transferred by gravity to barrel for fermentation in new French Oak. The result is a radiant color wine with lively golden hues. This Chardonnay is loaded with candied lemons and limes accompanied by hints of pear, cumquats, crushed rock and salt. Laser crisp and fresh.

# Mezzo Pollo al Limone

*roasted chicken with fresh lemon and herbs*

**SERVES 4**

4 chicken halves

Salt and pepper to taste

$\frac{1}{4}$ cup extra virgin olive oil

4 cloves garlic, whole

Small bunch of fresh rosemary, Italian parsley, sage and basil

2 lemons, peeled

$\frac{1}{2}$ yellow onion, sliced

3 cups chicken stock

4 slices prosciutto

4 tablespoons unsalted butter

PREHEAT OVEN TO 400 degrees F. Rub the chicken with salt and pepper, olive oil, garlic and herbs. Roast the chicken for 35 minutes. Remove from oven and add the remaining ingredients beneath the chicken. Continue roasting until chicken is moist and tender. Remove chicken and plate. Slightly reduce the juices left in the pan and pour over the chicken halves. Serve immediately.

## WINE SUGGESTION

*Rusack Vineyards Sangiovese, Santa Ynez Valley.* The great grape of the Chianti region of Italy, Sangiovese grows exceptionally well on the hillside slopes of Santa Barbara County's Ballard Canyon vineyards. The Rusack Sangiovese is a great example of California-style version of this Italian gem. Fruit forward and well balanced with aromas of and flavors of raspberries, currants, maple syrup and cocoa.

# AGNELLO CON OLIVE

*braised lamb with olives*

**SERVES 4**

¼ tablespoon extra virgin olive oil

1½ pounds lamb

1 cup all-purpose flour, for dusting

½ cup wine

Salt and pepper to taste

Pinch of oregano

1 lemon, zested

3 cups chicken stock, divided

¼ cup fresh lemon juice

¼ cup kalamata olives, pitted and whole

IN A SAUTÉ PAN, heat olive oil over high heat. Dust lamb in flour and cook for about 10 minutes until water has evaporated from lamb. Add the wine and let alcohol evaporate. Add salt, pepper, oregano, lemon zest and 2 cups chicken stock. Reduce heat and simmer for about 45 minutes. Add remaining stock a little at a time. Add lemon juice and olives and continue cooking 10 additional minutes, or until lamb is moist and tender. Serve immediately with Purée of Potato with Truffle, see page 152.

**WINE SUGGESTION**

*Artiste Winery "Kind of Blue."* Artiste's highly sought-after wines, labeled with gorgeous works of impressionist art, are limited productions of less than 300 cases each, and are exclusively available through Artiste Tasting Studio, Club Artiste and Artiste.com. "Kind of Blue" showcases scents of baked blueberries, blackberry glaze and vanilla along with layers of licorice, eucalyptus and violet. Concentrated and undeniably delicious.

# Costolette di maiale alla Valdostana

*pork chop with sage, prosciutto and melted fontina cheese*

**SERVES 4**

5 tablespoons butter, reserve
1 tablespoon for sauce
⅓ cup olive oil
4 (6- to 8-ounce) pork chops
1 cup flour, for dusting
1 cup Marsala wine
Small handful fresh sage leaves
Salt and pepper to taste
8 slices prosciutto
8 slices fontina cheese, thinly sliced

PREHEAT OVEN TO 375 degrees F. Meanwhile, in a large frying pan over medium-high heat, add the butter and olive oil. Dust each chop in flour and add to pan. Cook for 2 minutes on each side. Glaze the pan with the wine, sage, salt and pepper. Top each pork chop with a slice of prosciutto and a slice of fontina cheese. Remove pan from heat and bake in the preheated oven until cheese is melted. Remove from oven and place one chop on each serving plate. Using the remaining juices from the pan, reduce the sauce with the reserved butter and pour over each pork chop. Serve immediately.

**WINE SUGGESTION**

*Shoestring Winery Syrah.* Aged in French Oak barrels, this wine exhibits briar-patch fruit characteristics, namely a pronounced note of blackberries and boysenberries on the nose and mouth. Syrah lovers will enjoy its weight and structure. The texture and mouth-feel of this wine is warm and well balanced. The Shoestring Winery is located at the gateway of the beautiful Santa Ynez Valley of Santa Barbara County, California.

# SCALOPPINE AL PROSCIUTTO E CHAMPIGNON

*veal scaloppini with prosciutto and champignon mushrooms*

**SERVES 4**

¼ cup olive oil

8 (3-ounce) slices veal scaloppini (very thin), tenderize if necessary

1 cup flour, for dusting

8 slices prosciutto

8 slices fontina cheese

1 clove garlic

¼ pound champignon or porcini mushrooms, sliced

½ cup white wine

Salt and pepper to taste

1 cup chicken stock

3 tablespoons butter

1 tablespoon chopped fresh Italian parsley, for garnish

PREHEAT OVEN TO 400 degrees F. In a sauté pan over high heat, add the olive oil. Dust the scaloppini in flour and add to pan. Cook until golden brown on each side. Top each scaloppini with a slice of prosciutto and fontina cheese. Reserve in a baking dish. In the sauté pan, add the garlic, mushrooms, wine, salt, pepper, chicken stock and butter. Cook for about 5 minutes and pour over the veal scaloppini. Place the scaloppini in the oven and bake for about 15 minutes, or until cheese is melted. Top with Italian parsley and serve immediately.

## WINE SUGGESTION

*Carhartt Vineyard Estate Syrah, Santa Ynez Valley.* Carhartt Vineyard is a family-farmed vineyard and winery located in the center of the Santa Ynez Valley. Their estate Syrah is a big, focused wine with deeply concentrated flavors. The core reveals notes of dark red and blackberry fruit, chocolate and plum. The nose has dense red fruit aromas overlaid with meaty characteristics, earth, spice and leather. A well-structured wine, Carhartt's Syrah will age beautifully.

# SALTIMBOCCA DI SORRENTO

*sautéed pork loin with salami, parmesan and buffalo mozzarella*

**SERVES 4**

4 tablespoons butter

2 tablespoons olive oil

8 (3- to 4-ounce) slices pork loin, pounded thinly

Flour

½ cup white wine

Salt and pepper to taste

½ tablespoon oregano

8 slices salami Toscano

4 tablespoons grated Parmesan cheese

1 cup teardrop or cherry tomatoes, halved

8 basil leaves

8 slices fresh buffalo mozzarella

1 tablespoon chopped Italian parsley, for garnish

PREHEAT OVEN TO 400 degrees F. In a sauté pan, heat butter and oil over medium-high heat. Dust the pork loins with flour and add to pan. Cook until golden-brown on both sides. Remove from heat and add the wine, salt, pepper and oregano. Top each loin with 1 slice of salami, Parmesan cheese, tomato, basil and a slice of buffalo mozzarella. Place in oven and cook until cheese is melted. Serve immediately topped with Italian parsley.

## WINE SUGGESTION

*Dierberg Vineyard Pinot Noir, Santa María Valley.* A dark wine, Dierberg's Pinot Noir features aromas of wild sage, blackberry and some of the wild raspberry notes that characterize the vineyard. The varietal showcases a whiff of crushed red and green peppercorns and licorice. The blackberry theme continues on the palate with a firm structure and just enough acid to keep things fresh. The wine finishes very long.

# Costolette di Agnello alla Brace

*italian grilled rack of lamb with red wine reduction sauce*

**SERVES 4**

Salt and pepper to taste

2 racks of lamb

2 tablespoons chopped fresh rosemary

2 tablespoons chopped fresh sage

½ cup Dijon mustard

**RED WINE REDUCTION SAUCE**

¼ cup olive oil

4 cloves garlic

4 sprigs fresh rosemary

4 fresh sage leaves

½ cup red wine

2 tablespoons Dijon mustard

1 tablespoon beef paste

½ cup chicken stock

SALT AND PEPPER the racks of lamb. Mix herbs and mustard together and rub generously on the racks. Grill the lamb under the broiler or on an outdoor grill until medium-rare (or until your liking) and let rest for 10 minutes.

FOR THE SAUCE, prepare by heating olive oil in a small saucepan over medium-high heat. Add the garlic, rosemary and sage and cook for 1 minute. Add the red wine. Cook for another minute and add the mustard, beef paste and chicken stock; reduce the liquid by half. Remove the sauce from the heat. Cut lamb into chops and serve immediately with the wine reduction sauce and a side of Sautéed Spinach, see page 136.

## WINE SUGGESTION

*Bridlewood Estate Winery Reserve Syrah.* Sourced from vineyards in all regions of California's Central Coast, Bridlewood's Reserve Syrah is crafted in an old-world style of ripe fruit, earthy nuances and balanced tannic structure. Soft and succulent yet full-bodied with firm tannins, the Reserve Syrah is a mouth-watering wine with flavors of blackberry jam, plum and dark cherry fruit.

# NODINO DI VITELLO CON SPUGNOLE AL BRANDY

*sautéed veal chop with morel mushrooms and brandy*

**SERVES 4**

¼ cup olive oil

4 (10-ounce) veal chops

Salt and pepper to taste

¼ cup brandy

1 cup sliced morel mushrooms

2 tablespoons Dijon mustard

2 cups heavy cream

1 small bunch fresh thyme

½ cup chicken stock

1 tablespoon truffle oil

IN A SAUTÉ PAN over medium heat, add the olive oil and veal chops and cook each side for about 10 minutes. Add salt, pepper, brandy, mushrooms, Dijon mustard, cream, thyme and stock. Continue cooking until veal is cooked thoroughly and sauce is creamy. Remove from heat, plate the veal and top with the sauce. Drizzle with truffle oil just before serving.

**WINE SUGGESTION**

*Consilience Grenache, Rodney Shull Vineyard.* Consilience is a boutique winery in the beautiful Santa Ynez Valley of Santa Barbara County producing a variety of consistent and expressive wines with a loose focus on the traditional Rhône varietals. The Grenache is a rich, medium-bodied red wine with a unique rusticity and smoky character complementing lush flavors of cherry, black currant and blackberry. Perfect for pairing with veal, pork chops and maybe even a Montecristo No. 2.

# PATATE AL FORNO
*roasted potatoes*

**SERVES 4**

2 pounds Yukon gold potatoes, peeled
and diced

½ cup olive oil

Salt and pepper to taste

2 stems rosemary, roughly chopped

4 cloves garlic

PREHEAT OVEN TO 400 degrees F. In a bowl, add the potatoes, oil, salt, pepper, rosemary and garlic; mix well. Pour the potatoes into a roasting pan and cover with aluminum foil. Roast for about 45 minutes. Remove the foil and cook for another 15 minutes. Serve warm.


# PURÉ DI PATATE AL TARTUFO
*purée of potato with truffle*

**SERVES 4**

2 pounds russet potatoes, peeled
and large diced

2 tablespoons butter, melted

¾ cup milk, scalded

2 tablespoons mascarpone cheese

2 tablespoons grated Parmesan cheese

2 teaspoons truffle oil

Salt and pepper to taste

SIMMER THE POTATOES in salted water until tender; drain. Remove potatoes and place them in a mixing bowl. Whip the potatoes using an electric mixer on high speed for about 40 seconds. Scrape down the bowl and whip for an additional 30 seconds, eliminating all the lumps. Add the butter, milk, mascarpone and Parmesan cheese. Mix well on low speed. Add the truffle oil and season with salt and pepper. Serve warm.

# GRIGLIATA DI SPADA, GAMBERI E CALAMARI

*grilled swordfish with prawns and calamari*

**SERVES 4**

2 fresh swordfish fillets (U.S. caught),
cut in half

4 large prawns

4 whole calamari, cleaned

Salt and pepper to taste

1 lemon, juiced

4 tablespoons olive oil

1 tablespoon chopped Italian parsley

3 tablespoons extra virgin olive oil

1 tablespoon fresh lemon juice

MARINATE THE swordfish, prawns and calamari in a bowl with salt, pepper, lemon juice, olive oil and parsley. Turn on broiler or outdoor grill on medium-high heat. Place all the seafood on the grill and cook until tender and the swordfish is moist and flaky. In a small bowl whisk together extra virgin olive oil with fresh lemon juice and a dash of salt and pepper; set aside. Remove fish from heat and divide seafood equally on four plates. Top with the fresh parsley, oil and lemon sauce and serve immediately.

## WINE SUGGESTION

*Great Oaks Ranch & Vineyard Sauvignon Blanc, Santa Ynez Valley.* Sauvignon Blanc is quickly becoming the most important white variety in the Santa Ynez Valley. The fruit is cold fermented in a stainless-steel tank then aged in flavorless barrels before being bottled by gravity. This Sauvignon Blanc has the typical racy acidity associated with the varietal, complexed with lush tropical-citrus flavors.

# Gamberoni alla Toscana

*tuscan prawns with cannellini beans*

**SERVES 4**

6 large spot prawns (U.S.)

6 slices pancetta

⅓ cup olive oil

2 tablespoons butter

2 to 3 bunches fresh spinach

2 to 3 cloves garlic, chopped

Olive oil

Salt and pepper to taste

Pinch of chili flakes

12 ounces cannellini beans (cooked in jar)

2 to 3 sage leaves

Fresh Italian parsley, chopped

1 lemon, cut into wedges

WASH PRAWNS WITH cold water. Remove tail shell and devein. Leave head/body shell intact. Next, wrap a slice of pancetta around each section of tail meat. Secure with toothpick if necessary. In a hot skillet, add olive oil and butter (as needed) and sauté prawns for 1 to 2 minutes. Transfer skillet to a preheated oven and bake at 450 degrees for 15 minutes. While shrimp are baking, sauté fresh spinach with garlic, olive oil, salt, pepper, and chili flakes. When leaves become wilted, remove spinach from pan. In another skillet, sauté the beans with sage, another pinch of chili flakes and butter for 5 minutes. To serve, ladle some beans in center of plate. Place the sautéed spinach around the beans. Arrange 3 prawns in center of dish. Garnish with parsley and lemon wedges. Drizzle some olive oil over top just before serving.

## WINE SUGGESTION

*Alexander and Wayne Chardonnay, Careaga Canyon, Santa Barbara County.*
Alexander and Wayne's handcrafted wines are produced in small lots from estate-grown grapes grown in the coolest areas of Santa Barbara County. Their Careaga Canyon Chardonnay is aged in Oak barrels from France and America, and reflects both the fruit of the grapes and the oak and spice notes from the barrels. The result is a classic Chardonnay of richness, fruit and light-brown spices.

# PESCE SPADA ALLA PUTTANESCA
*swordfish puttanesca*

**SERVES 4**

¼ cup olive oil

3 cloves garlic, minced

2 tablespoons capers

5 anchovy fillets

16 kalamata olives, pitted

1 cup crushed canned tomatoes

Pinch of oregano

4 fresh basil leaves

Salt and pepper to taste

4 (4- to 6-ounce) fresh swordfish steaks
(U.S. caught), thin slices

1 tablespoon chopped Italian parsley

IN A SAUTÉ PAN over medium heat, add the olive oil. Then add garlic and cook until golden. Add the capers, anchovies, olives, tomatoes, oregano, basil, salt and pepper. Cook approximately 10 minutes. Meanwhile, under the broiler or on an outdoor grill, cook the swordfish over medium-high heat for several minutes on each side, or until fish is moist and flaky (be careful not to overcook). Remove fish from heat and plate. Top with the Puttanesca sauce and fresh parsley. Serve immediately.

**WINE SUGGESTION**

*Summerwood GSM (Paso Robles)*. Summerwood Winery produces very limited quantities of ultra-premium, opulent wines that are available exclusively from the Westside Paso Robles estate. This GSM is a dark ruby-hued, soft, fleshy, full-throttle Mediterranean-styled wine. Enjoy a vibrant mouthful of pepper, salt sea breezes, black currants, sweet cherries, spice and a hint of herbs.

# SCALOPPINE SAPORITE

*sautéed veal with kalamata olives, anchovies and white wine*

**SERVES 4**

¼ cup olive oil

8 (3-ounce) slices veal scaloppini (very thin),
tenderize if necessary

1 cup flour, for dusting

20 black kalamata olives, pitted

4 anchovy fillets

1 tablespoon chopped Italian parsley

2 tablespoons capers

½ cup white wine

Salt and pepper to taste

IN A SAUTÉ PAN, add the oil on high heat. Dust the veal in flour and add to pan. Cook until each side is golden brown. Remove the veal and set aside. In the sauté pan, combine the olives, anchovies, parsley, capers, wine, salt and pepper. Add the scaloppini back to the pan. Cook for about 5 minutes and serve immediately.

## WINE SUGGESTION

*Palmina Arneis, Honea Vineyard, Santa Ynez Valley.* An ancient grape that dates back to the fifteenth century, Arneis is best grown in regions with warm/hot days and cool fog-laden nights. A near perfect home for this unique Italian grape is at Honea Vineyard in the Santa Ynez Valley where the micro-climate and the long growing season produces grapes of classic character with a California "zing." A steely straw-like color invites a swirl unleashing aromas of honey and acacia followed by orchard fruit flavors.

# Trancio di Tonno con Spugnole
*ahi tuna with brandy and morel mushroom sauce*

**SERVES 4**

¼ cup olive oil

Salt and pepper taste

4 (6- to 8-ounce) fresh tuna steaks
(U.S./Worldwide Yellowfin), ahi-grade

1 cup flour, for dusting

1 tablespoon unsalted butter

½ cup sliced morel mushrooms

¼ cup brandy

1 cup heavy cream

2 tablespoons Dijon mustard

1 small bunch fresh thyme

¼ cup chicken stock

IN A SAUTÉ PAN over high heat, add olive oil. Sprinkle salt and pepper on the tuna then dust in flour and place in pan. Sear both sides for 1 to 2 minutes so edges are golden-brown but rare in the center. Remove fish from pan and set aside, keeping warm. In a sauté pan, add the butter, mushrooms and brandy (caution: may produce a flame). Allow alcohol to evaporate. Add cream, mustard, thyme and chicken stock; stir until creamy. Plate the tuna steak and top with the sauce.

## WINE SUGGESTION

*Koehler Winery Reserve Chardonnay.* This Chardonnay represents the epitome of what Koehler Winery can do—a 100% barrel-fermented Chardonnay aged in new Oak barrels. A unique style of wine, the Reserve Chardonnay offers wonderful tropical notes and floral flavors, which marry well with the oak impression from the new barrels. The oak also gives the varietal a slight vanilla nuance. A balanced wine in all aspects.

# Aragosta alla Griglia con Fagioli all'Uccelletto
*grilled lobster with sage & cannellini beans*

**SERVES 4**

4 large lobster tails (U.S./Australia spiny lobster or Maine lobster)

1 bunch fresh tarragon

Salt and pepper to taste

¼ cup extra virgin olive oil

3 tablespoons extra virgin olive oil

1 tablespoon fresh lemon juice

Dash of sea salt

**CANNELLINI BEANS**

3 tablespoons butter

12 fresh sage leaves

4 cloves garlic

2 cans (15 ounces each) cannellini beans with liquid

Salt to taste

Pinch of crushed red pepper

MARINATE THE LOBSTER with tarragon, salt, pepper and ¼ cup olive oil and set aside for 30 minutes. Turn grill to high heat. When ready, grill the lobster tails until moist and tender (careful to not overcook). Remove from heat and let tails rest for several minutes.

TO PREPARE cannellini beans, add butter and sage in a saucepan over medium-high heat. Stir for 1 minute and add the garlic, beans, salt and crushed red pepper. Cook for about 10 minutes or until beans are creamy.

TO SERVE the lobster, place a bed of cooked cannellini beans on each plate. Top with the lobster tail. Whisk together 3 tablespoons olive oil, 1 tablespoon lemon juice and a dash of sea salt. Drizzle over lobster tail and beans. Serve immediately.

## WINE SUGGESTION

*Gainey Vineyard Sauvignon Blanc, Santa Ynez Valley.* The current trend in New World Sauvignon Blanc is to cool-ferment the wine in stainless steel tanks to accentuate the variety's refreshing fruit-forward qualities. That's exactly what Gainey Vineyard does. Enjoy fresh, lush aromas of grapefruit, lime and sweet melon with subtle underlying scents of lemongrass, peppermint and spring flowers.

# Tonno in Agrodolce

*ahi tuna with sweet and sour sauce*

**SERVES 4**

¼ cup cooking oil, for onions

2 medium yellow onions, sliced

½ cup balsamic vinegar

¼ cup sugar

¼ cup chicken stock

¼ cup olive oil

Salt and pepper to taste

4 (6- to 8-ounce) fresh tuna steaks
(U.S./Worldwide Yellowfin), ahi-grade

¼ cup flour, for dusting

IN A SAUTÉ PAN over medium-high heat, add cooking oil and sliced onions. Cook until onions are soft and golden. Add balsamic vinegar, sugar and chicken stock. Continue cooking for approximately 15 minutes, stirring frequently. Remove from heat and set aside. In another sauté pan add olive oil, salt and pepper. Dust the tuna in flour and then salt and pepper and place in pan. Sear both sides for 1 to 2 minutes so edges are golden-brown but rare in the center. Remove fish from pan and top with the sweet and sour onion sauce.

**WINE SUGGESTION**

*Whitcraft Winery Bien Nacido Pinot Noir.* Whitcraft Winery continues to seek out new sources of the highest-quality grapes so they can deliver ever-improving products to their loyal clientele, those who have discovered through them that "Pinot Noir—it's not just for breakfast anymore! The featured Pinot is 100% Bien Nacido fruit. Wonderful berry fruit in the nose and mouth, sweet and lush on the tongue with a nice long finish. This wine is not to be missed.

# SOGLIOLE CON LIMONE E CAPPERI

*sautéed sole with lemons and capers*

**SERVES 4**

¼ cup olive oil

4 (6- to 7-ounce) fresh sole fillets
(Dover or Petrale)

1 cup flour, for dusting

1 cup white wine

Salt and pepper to taste

3 tablespoons capers

2 lemons, juiced

1 tablespoon chopped Italian parsley

IN A SAUTÉ PAN over medium-high heat, add the olive oil. Dust each fillet in flour and add to pan. Cook each side for about 5 minutes. Add the wine, salt, pepper, capers, lemon juice and parsley. Continue to cook for about 10 minutes, or until fish is moist and flaky and the wine is reduced. Serve immediately.

**WINE SUGGESTION**

*Ironstone Vineyards Viognier.* The main feature of the Ironstone Vineyards's Viognier is the complex aroma and flavors. With its distinctive tropical bouquet of citrus blossom, acacia and white melon, the Viognier leaves you day-dreaming about tropical faraway locations. Its lingering aroma eludes a sense of sweetness, but once on the palate, its rich mango and apricot flavors take hold. This full-bodied white has subtle spice notes with a long, full finish.

# POLLO ALLA CACCIATORA

*chicken cacciatora*

**SERVES 4**

¼ cup olive oil

1 whole chicken, cut into pieces

½ cup white wine

1 cup crushed tomatoes, canned

1 medium yellow onion, diced

1 cup chicken stock

1 clove garlic

1 tablespoon thyme

1 tablespoon basil leaves

1 tablespoon chopped Italian parsley

2 tablespoons capers

15 black kalamata olives, pitted and whole

HEAT OLIVE OIL in a roasting pan over medium-high heat. Add the chicken and cook for about 15 minutes, turning the pieces occasionally. Pour the wine over the chicken and add the remaining ingredients; stir well. Cover the pan and let simmer until chicken is tender and falls off the bone, about 45 minutes. Remove from heat and serve warm.

**WINE SUGGESTION**

*Arthur Earl Nebbiolo, Stolpman Vineyard, Santa Ynez Valley.* The Stolpman Vineyard in Santa Ynez has been producing Nebbiolo from here since 1997. The terrain is rolling to hilly with well drained soils and the climate has the ability to get this variety ripe every year. The cherry-red color found in every bottle is a hint of the black cherry flavors that dominate this Italian varietal. Perfect acidity level too.

# CIOPPINO ITALIANO

*classic italian fish and shellfish stew*

**SERVES 4**

⅓ cup extra virgin olive oil

1 medium yellow onion, sliced

4 cloves garlic, whole

1 pound black mussels

1 pound manila clams

1 pound calamari, sliced into rings

1 pound halibut (Pacific)

1 pound salmon (wild-caught)

4 basil leaves

Salt and pepper to taste

¼ cup white wine

Pinch of crushed red pepper

1 tablespoon oregano

1 cup chopped canned tomato

4 cups clam juice

1 pound large shrimp or prawns (U.S.), in shell

1 tablespoon chopped fresh Italian parsley

IN A LARGE STOCKPOT over high heat, add the olive oil, onion and garlic and cook for about 5 minutes, or until onion and garlic are soft and golden. Add all the seafood except the shrimp. Add the basil. Cook for about 4 minutes, then add the salt, pepper, wine, crushed red pepper and oregano. Cook for another 2 minutes. Add the tomatoes and clam juice. Reduce to medium heat, cover pot and cook for about 20 minutes, or until all the fish is tender and flaky. Add the shrimp to the pot several minutes before cooking is complete. Remove pot from heat and divide portions into four deep bowls. Top with parsley and serve with a slice of country bread and a wedge of lemon.

## WINE SUGGESTION

*Curtis Winery Heritage Cuvée, Santa Barbara County.* This Cuvée is a classic Rhône-style blend of Grenache (45%), Syrah (33%), Mourvédre (18%) and Cinsault (4%) from their estate vineyards in the Santa Ynez Valley. It begins with complex aromas of black fruits, sandalwood and spice. Vivid flavors of black cherry and blackberry unfold with accents of vanilla and tobacco. Texture is broad and balanced.

# SALMONE ALLA CHECCA

*roasted salmon with checca sauce*

**SERVES 4**

4 tablespoons extra virgin olive oil

4 fresh salmon steaks (wild-caught)

4 cloves garlic, whole

6 Roma tomatoes, diced, or cherry
tomatoes, halved

6 fresh basil leaves

¾ cup chicken stock

Salt and pepper to taste

IN A LARGE SKILLET, heat olive oil over medium heat. Add salmon fillets and cook each side for approximately 3 minutes. Add the garlic and cook for an additional minute. Add the tomatoes and basil and cook for 2 minutes more. Add the chicken stock, salt and pepper. Continue cooking until salmon is moist and flaky. Remove from heat and plate the salmon topped with the sauce from the skillet. Serve immediately.

### WINE SUGGESTION

*Lincourt Winery Chardonnay, Santa Barbara County.* The Lincourt Chardonnay is a distinct and complex wine with an amazing fruit-driven nature. The bouquet of aromas of mandarin orange, pineapple, pink grapefruit and mango are infused with notes of honeysuckle, vanilla, hazelnut and caramel. A clean wine with crisp acidity and coupled with round and creamy textures in the mouth.

# Ippoglosso al Balsamico

*halibut with balsamic soy sauce*

**SERVES 4**

4 (6- to 7-ounce) fresh halibut
steaks (Pacific)

Sea salt to taste

**SALSA BALSAMICO**

½ cup sugar

5 tablespoons soy sauce

½ cup balsamic vinegar

2 tablespoons cornstarch

1 yellow onion, sliced

SEASON THE HALIBUT steaks with sea salt and broil in oven or on outdoor grill over high heat until moist and flaky (do not overcook). In a saucepan, combine sugar, soy sauce, balsamic vinegar and cornstarch. Cook over medium heat for about 3 to 5 minutes. Add the sliced onion and cook for an additional 5 minutes. Dry the cooked halibut steaks with paper towels then top with the sauce and serve immediately with a side of Roasted Potatoes, see page 152.

## WINE SUGGESTION

*Fess Parker Viognier, Santa Barbara County.* The Fess Parker Winery and Vineyard farms almost 700 acres on four vineyards throughout Santa Barbara County. One of their signature varietals—Viognier—offers aromas of peach, honeysuckle, vanilla, apricot blossom, nutmeg and spice along with flavors of pineapple, ripe peach, lychee and citrus. Refreshing acidity and subtle oak makes this a nicely balanced Viognier.

# DECADENT DESSERTS

SWEETS DREAMS ON A PLATTER

Like the delicious entrées served at Trattoria Grappolo, the handcrafted desserts are equally divine. Each sweet surprise originates from a traditional recipe but is masterfully recreated and perfected to become a Grappolo original.

"I believe in offering a collection of rustic desserts that are informal and unpretentious," says Chef Leonardo Curti. "Our desserts reflect the simplicity and casualness found at our restaurant."

Grappolo's heavenly treats are continually rotated on the menu to ensure that the seasonality and freshness of ingredients always remains on the menu forefront.

The bistro's exquisite pear tart—dazzling orchard pears layered in a light, flaky crust and sprinkled with almond essence—bursts with aromas, flavors and vivid memories of family gatherings. So too does the restaurant's signature pastry: a melt-in-your-mouth flourless chocolate cake, rich and decadent, floating in a coffee cream anglaise. Other freshly-baked favorites are the crème brûlée infused with local California lavender, a refreshing light and sweet Panna Cotta, and the often requested Tiramisu, hand assembled with imported Italian ladyfingers, soaked in espresso and layered with whipped mascarpone cheese.

No matter what dessert you select, each pairs well with a fresh roasted cup of coffee, a hot espresso, a finely-aged port, or Chef Leonardo Curti's personal favorite: homemade *limoncello*, an iridescent yellow liqueur—thick and icy cold with an intense citrus bite.

# TORTA DI CIOCCOLATO

*rich decadent flourless chocolate cake with*
*mocha cream anglaise*

**SERVES 8**

½ cup water

2 sticks unsalted butter

1½ cups fine-quality semisweet or
bittersweet chocolate chips

1 cup fine sugar

2 teaspoons pure coffee extract

3 whole eggs

3 yolks

IN A SMALL SAUCEPAN, bring water and butter to a boil. In a mixer bowl with whisk attachment, add chocolate and sugar then immediately pour hot simmering butter mixture over chocolate. Add coffee extract and whisk on low. Stop and scrape the bottom. Turn on low and then add eggs (with yolks) only to blend.

NEXT, PREPARE EIGHT 4-ounce aluminum tin cups by placing them in a 9 x 13-inch baking dish. Spray each cup with nonstick spray and fill to the rim with the cake batter. Place dish in oven and pour in enough water to partially submerge tins, creating a water bath. Bake at 325 degrees F for 35 to 40 minutes, or until top of cakes are set. Cake may appear wet so test by touching the center of one cake. The cake will be done when no finger mark is made. Make sure cakes don't get puffy, otherwise it will overcook and have an egg-like flavor.

WHEN DONE, REMOVE cakes from oven and let cool. Then refrigerate cakes at least 4 hours before serving.

TO SERVE, REMOVE cakes from tins by inverting onto a plate. Serve with Mocha Anglaise sauce, see page 196, and fresh berries.

# SEMIFREDDO AL LIMONE
*frozen lemon mousse*

**MAKES 1 (8-INCH) ROUND SEMIFREDDO**

2 cups heavy whipping cream

½ cup sugar

1 tablespoon vanilla extract

2 cups lemon curd

1 lemon, zested

WHIP TOGETHER THE cream, sugar and vanilla until peaks form. Fold lemon curd into the cream and pour into an 8-inch springform pan. Freeze for at least 4 hours. Serve with lemon zest and Crèma Inglese, see page 196.

# RASPBERRY SAUCE

**MAKES APPROXIMATELY 14 OUNCES**

1 (12-ounce) bag frozen raspberries, thawed

1 teaspoon cornstarch

2 tablespoons sugar

1 teaspoon fresh lemon juice

USING A BLENDER or food processor, purée raspberries and strain; set aside. In a saucepan, whisk together cornstarch and sugar; add the strained raspberry purée. Bring to a boil over medium heat, stirring often. Reduce heat and continue cooking 1 additional minute. Remove from heat, add lemon juice and cool over an ice bath to stop the cooking process. Refrigerate until ready to use.

TO SERVE, pour the sauce into a squeeze bottle and drizzle sparingly onto dessert plates next to the dessert.

# Zuppa Inglese

*english trifle*

**SERVES 8**

**SIMPLE SYRUP**

¼ cup water

¼ cup sugar

½ cup sweet vermouth

**TRIFLE**

3 cups whole milk

6 tablespoons sugar, divided

Zest of ½ an orange

4 egg yolks

2 tablespoons cake flour

1 teaspoon vanilla extract

¼ cup semisweet chocolate chips

¼ cup Dutch cocoa powder, sifted

12 ladyfingers, broken in half

Chocolate, curled for garnish

8 strawberries, for garnish

**NOTE**

Have all ingredients ready and prepped because once cooking begins, the process is very fast.

MAKE SIMPLE SYRUP by bringing water and sugar to a boil and simmer for 1 minute. Remove from heat and slightly cool. Add vermouth and set aside.

IN A MEDIUM SAUCEPAN, bring milk, 3 tablespoons sugar, and orange zest to a simmer. In another bowl, whisk egg yolks and remaining sugar together, then add cake flour and whisk until completely smooth. Next, temper eggs with hot milk mixture by slowly pouring and whisking, then add back to pan on medium-low heat whisking constantly until thickened. Reduce heat and whisk an additional minute. Remove from heat and add the vanilla extract. Divide the custard mixture between two stainless steel bowls and to one of them, add chocolate chips and cocoa powder. Dip ladyfingers two at a time in the simple syrup and then place one ladyfinger in the bottom of each martini glass. Spoon all of the chocolate custard into the eight glasses, covering the ladyfinger. Dip remaining ladyfingers two at a time, and then place two in each glass. Spoon in the vanilla custard to cover the top. Refrigerate at least 2 hours before serving. Garnish with chocolate curls and a strawberry.

# TORTA DI RICOTTA

*citrus ricotta cheese cake*

**SERVES 8**

15 ounces ricotta cheese

½ cup sugar

Zest of 1 lemon

Zest of 1 orange

5 eggs, reserving whites in a mixing bowl

½ cup heavy cream

½ teaspoon vanilla extract

½ teaspoon pure orange extract

Pasta Frolla crust, unbaked (see below)

IN A MEDIUM MIXING bowl, add ricotta, sugar and zests. Use a spatula to smooth the cheese. Add egg yolks, cream and extracts. Whip reserved egg whites to a soft peak, then fold into cheese mixture. Pour into an 11-inch tart pan that has been prepared with a Pasta Frolla crust. Bake at 325 degrees F for 30 minutes, rotate pan 180 degrees, then bake an additional 30 minutes. When cooked, remove tart and refrigerate. When cool, cut into wedges and serve.

# PASTA FROLLA

*homemade pastry dough*

**MAKES 2 DOUGH BALLS**

3 cups all-purpose flour

2 teaspoons baking powder

1 cup sugar

1 teaspoon lemon zest

½ teaspoon salt

6 tablespoons butter, cold and cut into small cubes

3 eggs

¼ teaspoon vanilla extract

IN A FOOD PROCESSOR, pulse dry ingredients together. Add butter and pulse twelve times. Crack eggs into a measuring cup, turn on processor and add eggs and vanilla extract. Stop and then pulse ten times, or until crumbly. Empty contents onto counter and divide into two balls. Wrap the balls in plastic wrap and refrigerate at least 1 hour or up to 24 hours. Freeze dough if not planning to use within 24 hours.

TO MAKE CRUST, roll dough between two pieces of plastic wrap that have been slightly dusted with flour. Use bottom piece of plastic wrap to lift dough and transfer to an 11-inch tart pan that has been sprayed with nonstick spray and lined with parchment paper.

# MACEDONIA

*fruit cocktail*

**SERVES 4**

⅓ cup sugar

1 cup water

1 lemon, juiced

½ cup prosecco or dry white wine

2 cups fresh diced fruit (plums, kiwi, grapes, oranges, strawberries, etc.)

Vanilla ice cream and Crème Chantilly, as needed, for topping

Balsamic vinegar

IN A SMALL SAUCEPAN, combine sugar and water and bring to a simmer. When sugar has melted, remove from heat and let cool. When cool, add the lemon juice, prosecco or dry white wine, and diced fruit. Chill for at least 2 hours. Top with a scoop of vanilla ice cream, a dollop of Crème Chantilly, see page 187, and a drizzle of balsamic vinegar.

# PANNA COTTA

*italian creamy eggless sweet custard with caramel sauce*

**SERVES 8**

2 cups heavy cream

1 cup whole milk

¼ cup sugar

3 gelatin leaves

1 teaspoon vanilla extract

PLACE CREAM, MILK AND SUGAR in a large saucepan and bring to a simmer. Have gelatin leaves soaking in cold water. When cream comes to a simmer, remove from heat and add the strained gelatin leaves. Whisk slowly until gelatin is dissolved; add the vanilla. Pour cream mixture into eight 4-ounce plastic soufflé cups. Refrigerate at least 6 hours to set completely. Invert cup onto a single serving dish and serve with Caramel Sauce, see page 194.

# CREMA DI LAVANDA BRÛLÉE
*crème brûlée with california lavender*

**SERVES 8**

1 quart heavy cream

¾ cup granulated sugar

1 tablespoon dried lavender

10 egg yolks

½ cup whole milk

IN A MEDIUM SAUCEPAN, bring the cream, sugar and lavender to a simmer and then remove from heat. Next, whisk the egg yolks and milk into the heated cream mixture and strain through a fine strainer. Pour the mixture equally into eight 8-ounce ramekins that are arranged in a deep baking dish. Place in oven, and fill hot water to partially submerge ramekins. Bake at 320 degrees F for about 45 minutes, or until crème doesn't jiggle in the center. When cooked, remove ramekins and refrigerate at least 6 hours to set. To serve, sprinkle a layer of granulated sugar on top and caramelize with a kitchen torch.

# CRÈME CHANTILLY
*whipped cream*

**MAKES 2 CUPS**

2 cups heavy cream, chilled

2 tablespoons confectioners' sugar, sifted

1 teaspoon vanilla extract

USING AN ELECTRIC MIXER with a whisk attachment, whip cream until soft peaks form. Add sugar and vanilla and continue whipping until mixture starts to thicken. Remove contents and refrigerate until ready to use.

# Pere alla Finanziera

*almond cream pear tart with apricot glaze*

### SERVES 8

14 ounces almond paste

⅓ cup sugar

Zest from ⅓ of a lemon

1½ sticks unsalted butter, room temperature, cut into cubes

3 eggs

¼ teaspoon almond extract

⅓ cup all-purpose flour

4 canned pear halves, cut in half lengthwise

Powdered sugar

Crème Chantilly (see page 187)

Strawberries, for garnish

### APRICOT GLAZE

½ cup apricot jam

1 tablespoon water

USING A FOOD processor, pulse almond paste, sugar and zest. Transfer to a mixing bowl with a paddle attachment. Slowly add butter a little at a time; stop and scrape down sides. Turn machine on again and add eggs, one at a time, and then add almond extract and flour.

SPRAY EIGHT 4-OUNCE aluminum tin cups with nonstick spray and fill cups evenly. Pour in and smooth batter and place a slice of pear on top. Bake at 325 degrees F for 45 minutes, or until medium golden-brown. After cakes have cooled, glaze the tops with the Apricot Glaze. Dust with powdered sugar, fresh Crème Chantilly and a strawberry. Serve warm.

TO MAKE THE GLAZE, melt the apricot jam and water in a small saucepan. Pour through a strainer and brush evenly over cooled tarts.

# TIRAMISÚ

*italian ladyfingers soaked in espresso,*
*layered with whipped mascarpone cheese*

**SERVES 8**

1 cup espresso

1 cup Italian roast coffee

5 egg yolks

¾ cup sugar

1 (8-ounce) container mascarpone cheese

2 teaspoons marsala wine

2 cups heavy cream

2 teaspoons vanilla extract

24 ladyfingers

¼ cup Dutch cocoa powder

ADD BREWED COFFEES together and set aside to cool. Using an electric mixer with a whisk attachment, whisk egg yolks on low and slowly add the sugar. Turn mixer on medium-high and continue until thick and pale yellow in color. Add the mascarpone cheese until thoroughly mixed (stopping to scrape sides down if needed), then add marsala wine; set aside.

USING THE ELECTRIC MIXER with the whisk attachment, whip cream until soft peaks form, add vanilla, and continue to whisk until stiff peaks form. Fold into the mascarpone mixture; set aside.

DIP EACH LADYFINGER in the coffee mixture and completely cover the bottom of a 9 x 13-inch dish. Test the dessert dish by layering 12 (dry) ladyfingers in the dish to make sure they fit. Next, smooth over half of the cream mixture and repeat with another layer of coffee-soaked ladyfingers. Finish by spreading on remaining cream mixture. Refrigerate at least 4 hours. Before serving, dust with enough cocoa powder to completely cover the dessert.

# CROSTATA DI MELE CON GELATO DI VANIGLIA
*warm caramelized apple tart with vanilla gelato*

**SERVES 8**

1 stick unsalted butter

2 cups brown sugar

8 Granny Smith apples, peeled and cut into thirds, tossed with juice of 1 lemon

Pinch of cinnamon and salt

2 puff pastry sheets

Vanilla gelato or ice cream

PLACE EIGHT 8-OUNCE ramekins on a baking sheet. Preheat oven to 400 degrees F. Using a large sauté pan, melt butter over medium heat. Add brown sugar, stirring constantly to create a smooth sauce. Bring to a boil then add apples, stirring constantly to coat, for about 2 minutes. Remove from heat and add a pinch of cinnamon and salt. Thaw puff pastry about 5 minutes, then cut out 8 circles the size of the ramekins. Place 3 pieces of apples in each dish with the inside of the apples facing up. Strain juices and pour into ramekins to fill one-fourth of the ramekin. Place a piece of puff pastry on top of each dish. Bake until golden brown, about 20 minutes. Serve warm with vanilla gelato or ice cream.

# CARAMEL SAUCE

**MAKES 1 QUART**

4 cups sugar

4 cups water

2 cups heavy cream, room temperature but not warm

1 teaspoon fresh lemon juice

1 cup whole milk

1 teaspoon vanilla extract

Pinch of salt

COMBINE THE SUGAR and water in a 2-quart saucepan. Stir to dissolve sugar only. Stop stirring and use a clean wet pastry brush to wash down any sugar crystals on the sides of the pan. Do this every few minutes. Turn heat on high and boil until a dark amber color is achieved. Slightly swirl the pan to even the cooking.

REDUCE HEAT TO LOW. Slowly add the cream while stirring. Remove from heat and add the lemon juice, milk, vanilla and salt. Strain into a stainless container and stir periodically until cool. Cover with plastic wrap and refrigerate up to 1 week.

# CRÈMA INGLESE

*english cream sauce*

**MAKES 2¼ CUPS**

1 cup whole milk

1 cup heavy cream

¼ cup sugar

¼ vanilla bean, scraped into sugar

4 large egg yolks

¼ cup sugar

½ teaspoon pure vanilla extract

IN A MEDIUM saucepan, bring milk, cream, ¼ cup sugar, and vanilla bean to a boil. In a small bowl, whisk together egg yolks and ¼ cup sugar. Temper eggs by whisking in some of the hot cream, then return to saucepan and continue cooking over medium-low heat, using a heatproof spatula. Stir slowly until thickened (to coat the back of a spoon).

REMOVE FROM heat and pour through a strainer into another container placed over an ice bath. Add vanilla extract and stir often to cool. Cover with plastic wrap and allow to cool completely. Sauce is ready after chilling and will last in the refrigerator up to 1 week.

FOR MOCHA ANGLAISE, add 1 tablespoon coffee extract when adding the vanilla extract.

FOR ORANGE ANGLAISE, add zest of 1 orange when bringing milk to a boil.

# Torta Della Nonna
*grandmother cake*

**SERVES 8**

1 double crust Pasta Frolla (see page 183)

Vanilla and Lemon Crème Patisserie (see page 205)

¼ cup mini semisweet chocolate chips

1 egg, separated into two small bowls

1 tablespoon pine nuts

Confectioners' sugar

USING AN 11-INCH false bottom scalloped tart pan, spray with nonstick spray and line with parchment paper; place pan on a baking sheet. Mold the Pasta Frolla crust in the tart pan without removing the edges. Pour and spread the chilled pastry cream into the pan and sprinkle the chocolate chips on top. Brush edges of the crust with the beaten egg white, then fold over the crust to form a top. Press the edges to form a sealed scalloped edge and remove overhang. Next, beat the egg yolk with 1 teaspoon water and then lightly brush the top and sprinkle with pine nuts. Bake at 350 degrees F for 45 minutes. Remove from oven and let cool in pan. Veil with confectioners' sugar before serving.

# Mousse di Cioccolato
*chocolate mousse*

**SERVES 4-6**

1½ cups semisweet or bittersweet chocolate

2 cups heavy cream

4 egg whites, at room temperature

3 tablespoons sugar

IN A LARGE STAINLESS bowl, melt chocolate using a double boiler or water bath over medium heat. When chocolate is melted, remove from heat and set aside. Next, using an electric mixer, whip cream to stiff peaks; set aside. Whip egg whites until foamy and then add the sugar to the egg whites and whip to create stiff peaks. Next, rapidly whisk one-fourth of the whipped cream into the melted chocolate until blended. Fold the whipped egg whites into the chocolate along with the remaining cream. Put the prepared mousse into a storage container and refrigerate at least 4 hours, preferably overnight. To serve, pipe mousse into glasses and top with Crème Chantilly, see page 187, and a strawberry.

# Torta di Gianduia con Salsa di Lamponi

*gianduia chocolate truffle tart with raspberry sauce*

**SERVES 8**

¼ cup hazelnuts, whole, skinned and toasted

¼ cup Dutch cocoa powder

¼ cup sugar

1¼ cups all-purpose flour

¼ teaspoon salt

1 stick unsalted butter, cold and cubed

1 egg

**FILLING**

1 pound Gianduia chocolate, chopped into small pieces

1 stick unsalted butter, at room temperature and cubed'

1¼ cups heavy cream

IN A FOOD PROCESSOR, add hazelnuts and then turn on machine for 10 seconds. Add cocoa, sugar, flour, salt and butter; pulse about ten times. Turn on again and add the egg, then turn off; pulse about twelve times. Next, pour contents onto counter and work into a disk shape. Cover with plastic wrap and refrigerate at least 30 minutes or up to 24 hours. If not using right away, freeze up to 2 weeks.

WHEN READY, place an 11-inch tart pan on a baking sheet and prepare tart pan by lightly spraying with nonstick spray. Using a parchment round to line the pan, roll out dough between two pieces of plastic wrap and use bottom piece to lift dough onto the tart pan. Use excess dough to thicken the sides. Refrigerate for about 15 minutes, then bake at 350 degrees F for 15 minutes. When cooked, remove from oven and let cool before adding filling.

TO MAKE THE FILLING, place chocolate and butter in a medium-size stainless steel bowl. Next, bring the cream to a hard boil and pour over the chocolate and butter. Let set for 1 minute, then whisk and pour into the pre-baked shell and refrigerate for at least 4 hours. Serve with Raspberry Sauce, see page 181.

# FRAGOLINO

*homemade strawberry liqueur*

**MAKES APPROXIMATELY 1 LITER**

1 cup Everclear, or similar grain alcohol

10 to 12 fresh strawberries, wash, dried
and de-stemmed

1½ cups water

1 cup sugar

IN A MASON JAR, add the alcohol and strawberries. Store sealed for 1 week. Shake jar once a day. When ready, bring water to a boil and add sugar until melted, stirring constantly. Remove from heat and set aside to cool. Strain the alcohol and discard the strawberries. Add the alcohol to the cooled sugar mixture. Mix well, and store in a glass bottle or new mason jar. Keep in a cool dark place for a few days. Store the bottle or jar in the freezer until ready to serve.

# LIMONCELLO

*homemade citrus liqueur*

**MAKES APPROXIMATELY 1 LITER**

1 cup Everclear, or similar grain alcohol

5 organic lemons, peel only

1½ cups water

1 cup sugar

IN A MASON JAR, add alcohol and lemon peels (yellow part only). Let sit for 1 week. Shake jar once a day. When ready, bring water to a boil and add sugar until melted, stirring constantly. Remove from heat and set aside to cool. Strain the alcohol and discard the lemon peels. Add the alcohol to the cooled sugar mixture. Mix well, and store in a glass bottle or new mason jar. Keep in a cool dark place for a few days. Store the bottle or jar in the freezer until ready to serve.

# Canarino alla Menta

*lemon mint tea*

**SERVES 4**

4 lemons, peeled

4 small bunches fresh mint

4 cups hot water

4 tablespoons honey

DIVIDE THE lemon peel and mint into four highball glasses and then fill each with 1 cup hot water and 1 tablespoon honey. Let steep for 2 or 3 minutes before serving. This is a fantastic beverage to be enjoyed after a heavy meal, when feeling under the weather, or simply as an alternative to coffee or tea.

# Pastiera di Grano

*easter wheat pie*

**SERVES 8**

Pasta Frolla (see page 183)

½ cup whole milk

1 can presoaked wheat (about 15 ounces)

Pinch of salt

¼ cup minced citron fruit

1 teaspoon orange zest

1 cup sugar

1 pound ricotta cheese

4 eggs, separated

1 teaspoon orange flower water

1 teaspoon vanilla

Powdered sugar, for garnish

PREPARE AN 11-INCH tart pan bottom with the Pasta Frolla crust; set aside. In a small saucepan, scald milk and then add wheat while stirring constantly. Add the salt and cook for 5 minutes. Remove from heat and add the citron fruit and orange zest; set aside to cool.

IN A MEDIUM BOWL, mix sugar into the ricotta cheese until smooth, then add the egg yolks, orange flower water and vanilla. Stir wheat into the ricotta mixture. Whip egg whites to a soft peak and fold into the ricotta wheat mixture. Pour into the prepared tart pan and place on lattice strips (prepared by trimming and rolling remaining Pasta Frolla dough into strips). Press with fingers to adhere lattice to edge. Remove the overhang. Place tart on a baking sheet and bake at 350 degrees F for 30 minutes. Rotate and bake for an additional 30 minutes, or until lattice is golden brown. Serve at room temperature with a dusting of powdered sugar.

# CRÈME PASTICCIERA

*homemade pastry cream*

**MAKES ABOUT 2 CUPS**

2 large eggs

2 large egg yolks

¼ cup sugar

2 tablespoons cornstarch

2 tablespoons cake flour

2 cups whole milk

¼ cup sugar

2 tablespoons butter, at room temperature

2 teaspoons vanilla

IN A MEDIUM stainless steel bowl, whisk together eggs (with yolks) and ¼ cup sugar. Add cornstarch and cake flour, which have been sifted together, and whisk until all the lumps have been removed; set aside. Next, bring milk and ¼ cup sugar to a boil, temper with the eggs (achieved by slowly pouring the boiled milk into the egg mixture), and strain back into the saucepan. Whisk until thickened and return to a boil. Remove from heat and transfer contents into a clean bowl over an ice bath while stirring to help cool. Finally, add the butter and vanilla.

**OTHER CRÈME FLAVORS**

- Chocolate Crème, add 4 ounces bittersweet chocolate before ice bath.
- Coffee Crème, add 4 ounces coffee extract in place of or with vanilla.
- Raspberry Crème, add ⅓ cup raspberry purée after cream cools slightly.
- Lemon or Orange Crème, steep zest of 1 orange or 1 lemon into milk.
- Vanilla Bean Crème, steep ½ of a vanilla bean in milk, then strain when tempering with eggs.

CALIFORNIA WINE CELLAR

We've all heard the age-old saying "white wine with fish, red wine with meat." After sitting down with a number of California winemakers, it appears the infamous adage doesn't hold much merit today. With fanciful restaurants like Trattoria Grappolo serving exquisite dishes punctuated with multiple ingredients and masterful side dishes, chefs such as Leonardo Curti are letting their dining guests in on a little secret: the key to proper wine selection is to choose a varietal based on the predominant flavors of the dish and not the specific food.

"What one must do is first look at all of the ingredients and flavors of the dish," says Chef Leonardo Curti. "A Pinot Noir with a little oak and a good amount of fruit will complement the flavors of say sweet peppers, spices and Parma ham. If Pinot isn't your preference, then try a crisp Chardonnay, but make sure there's enough acidity to play off the ham."

At Grappolo, wine education and selection is just as important as the food—and pairing the two is simple when Chef Leonardo and co-owner Daniele Serra are at the helm. "Let's say a dinner patron preorders a bottle of wine," says Serra, who manages Grappolo's cellar and offers daily recommendations to customers. "Our wait staff will relay this information to the kitchen and we will alter the dish to perfectly match it with the wine they have chosen. Alternatively, if the food is chosen first, then our knowledgeable staff or I will recommend several wine options to our guests. Either way, diners will have a perfectly paired dish ready to enjoy."

It is also worth noting that the extensive wine list has been carefully developed by Serra to ensure each showcased varietal will pair well with the entrées being offered.

Like chefs who continually experiment with food and wine pairings, so should the home cook or dinner guest. Try various whites and reds and see what you like best. To assist you, Chef Leonardo Curti, Daniele Serra and the supporting wineries in this book have suggested a fine wine to pair with many of the dishes. For those residing outside California who may not be able to locate a particular wine, many if not all the featured wineries ship nationwide. To assist you further, the following pages provide contact information for reaching the wineries directly.

**ALEXANDER & WAYNE WINERY**
2923 Grand Avenue
Los Olivos, CA 93441
805.688.9665
www.alexanderandwayne.com

**ARBIOS CELLARS**
561 Mission Boulevard
Santa Rosa, CA 95409
707.539.5641
www.arbioscellars.com

**ARTHUR EARL WINERY**
2921 Grand Avenue
Los Olivos, CA 93441
805.693.1771
www.arthurearl.com

**ARTISTE WINERY**
3569 Sagunto Street, Studio 102
Santa Ynez, CA 93460
805.686.2626
www.artiste.com

**BRANDER VINEYARDS**
2401 North Refugio
Los Olivos, CA 93441
805.688.2455
www.brander.com

**BRIDLEWOOD WINERY**
3555 Roblar Avenue
Santa Ynez, CA 93460
805.688.9000
www.bridlewoodwinery.com

**BUTTONWOOD FARM WINERY
& VINEYARD**
1500 Alamo Pintado
Solvang, CA 93463
805.688.3032
www.buttonwoodwinery.com

**CARHARTT VINEYARD & WINERY**
1691 Alamo Pintado Road
Solvang, CA 93463
805.688.0685
www.carharttvineyard.com

**CARINA CELLARS**
2900 Grand Avenue,
P.O. Box 644
Los Olivos, CA 93441
805.688.2459
www.carinacellars.com

**CASTORO CELLARS**
1315 North Bethel Road
Templeton, CA 93465
805.238.0725
www.castorocellars.com

**CHAPPELLET WINERY**
1581 Sage Canyon Road
St. Helena, CA 94574
707.963.7136
www.chappellet.com

**CHÂTEAU JULIEN WINE ESTATE**
8940 Carmel Valley Road
Carmel, CA 93923
831.624.2600
www.chateaujulien.com

**CONSILIENCE**
2933 Grand Avenue
Los Olivos, CA 93441
805.691.1020
www.consilience.com

**CURTIS WINERY**
5249 Foxen Canyon Road
Los Olivos, CA 93441
805.686.8999
www.curtiswinery.com

**DELOACH VINEYARDS**
1791 Olivet Road
Santa Rosa, CA 95401
707.526.9111
www.deloachvineyards.com

**DIERBERG ESTATE VINEYARD**
P.O. Box 1882
Santa Ynez, CA 93460
805.693.0744
www.dierbergvineyard.com

**DRY CREEK VINEYARD**
3770 Lambert Bridge Road
Healdsburg, CA 95448
800.864.9463
www.drycreekvineyard.com

**EBERLE WINERY**
P.O. Box 2459
Paso Robles, CA 93447
805.238.9607
www.eberlewinery.com

**EOS ESTATE WINERY**
5625 Highway 46 East
Paso Robles, CA 93446
805.239.2562
www.eosvintage.com

**FESS PARKER WINERY & VINEYARD**
6200 Foxen Canyon Road
Los Olivos, CA 93441
805.688.1545
www.fessparker.com

**FIRESTONE VINEYARD**
5000 Zaca Station Road
Los Olivos, CA 93441
805.688.3940
www.firestonewine.com

**FLORA SPRINGS WINERY
& VINEYARDS**
1978 West Zinfandel Lane
St. Helena, CA 94574
707.963.5711
www.florasprings.com

**FLYING GOAT CELLARS**
P.O. Box 1604
Santa Ynez, CA 93460
805.688.1814
www.flyinggoatcellars.com

**FOLEY ESTATES VINEYARD &
WINERY – RANCHO SANTA ROSA**
6121 East Highway 246
Lompoc, CA 93436
805.737.6222
www.foleywines.com

**FOPPIANO VINEYARDS**
P.O. Box 606
Healdsburg, CA 95448
707.433.7272
www.foppiano.com

**FOXEN WINERY & VINEYARD**
7200 Foxen Canyon Road
Santa Maria, CA 93454
805.937.4251
www.foxenvineyard.com

**GAINEY VINEYARDS**
3950 East Highway 246
Santa Ynez, CA 93460
805.688.0558
www.gaineyvineyard.com

**GALANTE VINEYARDS & WINERY**
18181 Cachagua Road
Carmel Valley, CA 93924
800.GALANTE
www.galantevineyards.com

**GREAT OAKS RANCH VINEYARD**
2450 Calzada Avenue
Santa Ynez, CA 93460
805.686.0895
www.greatoaksranch.com

**HAHN ESTATES / SMITH & HOOK WINERY**
37700 Foothill Road
Soledad, CA 93960
831.678.4555
www.hahnestates.com

**HUBER CELLARS**
1539 Mission Drive, Unit A
Solvang, CA 93463
805.686.9323
www.hubercellars.com

**IRONSTONE VINEYARDS**
1894 Six Mile Road
Murphys, CA 95247
209.728.1251
www.ironstonevineyards.com

**J. VINEYARDS & WINERY**
11447 Old Redwood Highway
Healdsburg, CA 95448
888.JWINECO
www.jwine.com

**J. WILKES WINE**
342 Oliver Road
Santa Barbara, CA 93109
805.899.2845
www.jwilkeswine.com

**KALYRA WINERY**
343 North Refugio Road
Santa Ynez, CA 93460
805.693.8864
www.kalyrawinery.com

**KOEHLER WINERY**
5360 Foxen Canyon Road
Los Olivos, CA 93441
805.693.8384
www.koehlerwinery.com

**LINCOURT VINEYARDS**
1711 Alamo Pintado Road
Solvang, CA 93463
805.688.8554
www.lincourtwines.com

**LUCAS & LEWELLEN VINEYARDS**
1645 Copenhagen Drive
Solvang, CA 93463
805.686.9336
www.llwine.com

**MANDOLINA WINERY**
1665 Copenhagen Drive
Solvang, CA 93463
805.686.5506
www.mandolinawinery.com

**MAURITSON WINES**
2859 Dry Creek Road
Healdsburg, CA 95448
707.431.0804
www.mauritsonwines.com

**MELVILLE VINEYARDS & WINERY**
5185 East Highway 246
Lompoc, CA 93436
805.735.7030
www.melvillewinery.com

**MONTICELLO VINEYARDS**
Corley Family Napa Valley
4242 Big Ranch Road
Napa, CA 94558
707.253.2802
www.corleyfamilynapavalley.com

**MOSBY WINERY & VINEYARDS**
P.O. Box 1849
Buellton, CA 93427
800.70.MOSBY
www.mosbywines.com

**OPTIMA WINERY**
498 "C" Moore Lane
Healdsburg, CA 95448
707.431.8222
www.optimawinery.com

**PALMINA WINES**
1520 East Chesnut Court
Lompoc, CA 93436
805.735.2030
www.palminawines.com

**PARADISE RIDGE FAMILY
ESTATE WINERY**
4545 Thomas Lake Harris Drive
Santa Rosa, CA 95403
707.528.9463
www.paradiseridgewinery.com

**PARAISO VINEYARDS**
38060 Paraiso Springs Road
Soledad, CA 93960
831.678.0300
www.paraisovineyards.com

**RANCHO SISQUOC WINERY**
6600 Foxen Canyon Road
Santa Maria, CA 93454
805.934.4332
www.ranchosisquoc.com

**RIDEAU VINEYARD**
1562 Alamo Pintado Road
Solvang, CA 93463
805.688.0717
www.rideauvineyard.com

**ROBERT HALL WINERY**
3443 Mill Road
Paso Robles, CA 93446
805.239.1616
www.roberthallwinery.com

**ROYAL OAKS / ROBLAR WINERY**
1651 Copenhagen Drive
Solvang, CA 93463
805.693.1740
www.royaloakswinery.com

**RUSACK VINEYARDS**
1819 Ballard Canyon Road
Solvang, CA 93463
805.688.1278
www.rusackvineyards.com

**RUTHERFORD GROVE WINERY
& VINEYARDS**
1673 Highway 29
Rutherford, CA 94573
707.963.0544
www.rutherfordgrove.com

**SHOESTRING VINEYARD & WINERY**
800 East Highway 246
Solvang, CA 93463
800.693.8612
www.shoestringwinery.com

**SUMMERWOOD WINERY & INN**
2175 Arbor Road
Paso Robles, CA 93446
805.227.1365
www.summerwoodwine.com

**SUNCÉ WINERY & VINEYARD**
1839 Olivet Road
Santa Rosa, CA 95401
707.526.WINE
www.suncewinery.com

**SUNSTONE VINEYARDS & WINERY**
125 Refugio Road
Santa Ynez, CA 93460
800.313.9463
www.sunstonewinery.com

**ST. SUPÉRY VINEYARDS & WINERY**
8440 St. Helena Highway
Rutherford, CA 94573
707.963.4507
www.stsupery.com

**TRENTADUE WINERY**
19170 Geyserville Avenue
Geyserville, CA 95441
707.433.3104
www.trentadue.com

**VJB VINEYARDS & CELLARS**
9077 Sonoma Highway
Kenwood, CA 95452
707.833.2300
www.vjbcellars.com

**WHITCRAFT WINERY**
36 A S. Calle Cesar Chavez
Santa Barbara, CA 93101
805.965.0956
www.whitcraftwinery.com

**WHITEHALL LANE WINERY**
1563 St. Helena Highway
St. Helena, CA 94574
800.963.9454
www.whitehalllane.com

**WILD COYOTE WINERY**
3775 Adelaida Road
Paso Robles, CA 93446
805.610.1311
www.wildcoyote.biz

**WILDHURST VINEYARDS**
3855 Main Street
Kelseyville, CA 95451
800.595.WINE
www.wildhurst.com

**WILLIAM JAMES CELLARS**
Santa Maria, CA
805.478.9412
www.williamjamescellars.com

2875 Woodstock Road
Santa Ynez, CA 93460

**ZACA MESA WINERY**
6905 Foxen Canyon Road
Los Olivos, CA 93441
805.688.9339
www.zacamesa.com

# ACKNOWLEDGMENTS

Chef Leonardo Curti and author James O. Fraioli would like to personally thank the following individuals for their generous support and assistance with this book:

Gibbs Smith, Melissa Barlow, and the entire staff at Gibbs Smith, Publisher; food photographer extraordinaire Luca Trovato and his talented wife and food stylist Rori Trovato; photographer Brian Hodges for taking such beautiful images of the restaurant; the wonderful staff at Trattoria Grappolo: Daniele Serra (co-owner), Chef Alfonso Curti; Chef Giorgio Curti; Alejandro Alba, Leonardo Casimiro, Fabian Castillo, Ismael Castillo, Javier Castillo, Martin De La Cruz, Armando Flores, Samuel Flores, Narisco L. Guadalupe, Gustavo V. Lopez, Michelle Mancuso, Medina Andres, Pedro Paque, Luis Perez, Santiago Rosales, Eric Rustrian, Dawn Stockwell and Blanca Velasco; Jennifer Curti; Sophia, Isabella and Camilla; Luigi Antonio Curti and Maria Santoro; Linda Vathayanon, Mauro Luppoli and Marcello Luppoli; Cindy Fraioli, Rachelle Raymond, Tish Raymond, Jim and Karin Fraioli, Sage of Santa Ynez, and all the participating wineries, which were a pleasure to work with.

## PHOTO CREDITS

Food photography provided by Luca Trovato
Restaurant & lifestyle photography provided by Brian Hodges

Other photography provided by:

Page 21 (family portrait), Michelle Warren Photography
Page 135, Jason Egbert
Page 191, Gibbs Smith, Publisher
Page 206 (grapes), Gibbs Smith, Publisher
Page 208–9, Bridlewood Winery
Page 210–11, Zaca Mesa Winery
Page 212–13 Melville Winery & Kirk Irwin—I&I Images
Page 214–15, Summerwood Winery & Chris Leschinsky

# INDEX